# Holiness and Sexuality

# Holiness and Sexuality

## Homosexuality in a Biblical Context

### Papers from the Seventh Oak Hill College Annual School of Theology

**Edited by David Peterson**

**PATERNOSTER**

First published in 2004 by Paternoster Press

10  09  08  07  06  05  04     7  6  5  4  3  2  1

Paternoster Press is an imprint of Authentic Media,
9 Holdom Avenue, Bletchley, Milton Keynes, MK1 1QR, UK
and Box 1047, Waynesboro, GA 30830-2047, USA
www.authenticmedia.co.uk

**British Library Cataloguing in Publication Data**

A catalogue record for this book is available from the British Library

ISBN 1-84227-269-1

Cover Design by 4-9-0 ltd
Print Management by Adare Carwin
Printed and bound in Denmark by Nørhaven Paperback A/S, Viborg

# Contents

# Foreword

The emotional heat engendered by the current controversies surrounding homosexuality and Christianity has not been conducive to serious thinking on the subject. The media has not helped either, often reporting sound bites rather than arguments. There is an urgent need for studies like this which help Christians to make a mature, robust and compassionate response to homosexuality in our culture, our churches and in many individual lives. It has all the right emphases: God, Scripture and people.

Too many approaches to this subject begin with a particular understanding of the phenomenon of homosexuality and argue from that base. But we must surely begin with God. What is the Creator's will for sexuality? How has that perfect pattern been spoilt by human rejection of God at the Fall? How does the Holy God want his redeemed people to live since the coming of Christ our Saviour? For the answers to all these questions, we must turn to God's word in the Scriptures. As we do so, we should not simply look for proof texts, but rather be prepared to do the hard work of responsible exegesis, taking into account the unfolding nature of God's revelation, as modelled by the contributors to this volume.

But, even then, our work is still not done. Good theology will not start with human experience, but it will certainly listen to it and speak into it. Homosexuality is not simply an 'issue'; it concerns people, created and loved by God. We should do all we can to understand, not just the Bible, but one another, so that we can lovingly reach out to those who do not know Christ, and support our fellow believers in the hard and joyful life of discipleship.

*Vaughan Roberts*
*St Ebbe's Church, Oxford*

# Introduction

With the current outpouring of books about homosexuality, it may seem hard to justify another contribution to the debate. However, many Christians remain confused about the way in which various church leaders differently interpret both the biblical and medical evidence. Some fundamental questions still need to be asked. What sort of theological and ethical framework should we adopt for assessing, integrating, and applying the biblical material? What is the status of medical theories most recently publicized and what are their ethical implications? What pastoral issues should we be addressing in our churches?

Denominational moves to authorize the blessing of same-sex unions or to permit those who are engaged in such unions to be church leaders have certainly raised the temperature of the debate in recent months. Advocates of the liberal agenda have been vigorous in putting their case, and they are often quite dismissive of those who oppose them. Their arguments need to be carefully weighed and evaluated. Those who want to maintain a conservative position cannot avoid being actively involved in this intellectual engagement. It is hoped that this book will enable them to do so with fresh insight and renewed confidence. At the same time, we need pastoral sensitivity, humility, and compassion in dealing with the many manifestations of our own sexual fallenness.

The present volume arises from a series of public presentations at the Annual School of Theology for clergy and other full-time workers, held at Oak Hill College, London, on April 30, 2003. The papers were revised in the light of feedback received on the day and after further research and reflection on the part of the contributors. A chapter has been added to engage more specifically with the issue of same-sex unions and the interpretation of Romans.

As to its contents, the book differs from other publications in several ways. Homosexuality is first considered within the context of the Bible's teaching about holiness and sexuality more generally. Two of the chapters I have written explore the link between these themes in biblical theology and respond to frequently asked questions about the legitimacy of using Old Testament material in a Christian context. These chapters address the particular charge about the selective use of Old Testament material with regard to sexuality. Holiness is shown to be an important interpretative key for evaluating and integrating biblical teaching on sexuality. Holiness also offers a helpful pastoral framework for applying Scripture in the contemporary scene.

The first three chapters also investigate whether the argument that the Bible is concerned only with exploitative or promiscuous same-sex unions has any validity. A key question here is whether Scripture allows for the possibility of permanent and stable homosexual unions. Chapter 3 specifically engages with the arguments of Jeffrey John and others on this topic.

A further distinctive of this book is the place given to two chapters of theological and ethical analysis, with the title "Radical Disorientation: Fallen Sexuality and the Christian Doctrine of Sin." David Field, who teaches doctrine and ethics at Oak Hill, offers a challenging perspective on sin as theologically defined. Viewing our fallen sexuality in this context "serves both to clarify and confirm our understanding of sin and also to provide fresh perspectives upon the radical disorientation that is, and that leads to fallen sexuality." The relationship between orientation and behavior is of particular importance in considering the sins of same-sex sexual activity. David argues in his second chapter that if God is "one and many," and sin is theologically defined, then "sin too will be one and many." The chapter explores the theological and pastoral implications of this argument and makes the point that "since sin is a God-problem, it is amenable only to a God-solution."

We often hear the challenge to listen to what homosexuals are saying. But so often the voices are strident and radical, demanding freedom of expression for their sexuality and the blessing of church leaders on their behavior. Martin Hallett contributes a chapter to this volume entitled "Homosexuality: Handicap and Gift." He writes as a homosexual Christian who is single and celibate, describing his own struggle and the difficulties faced by others in a similar position.[1] He views his sexuality in a positive way and seeks to use it in ministry to others, particularly in his role as the director of True freedom Trust. This is a Christian counseling and teaching organization in the United Kingdom, "offering hope and help to men and women struggling with homosexuality, lesbianism and related problems."[2] Martin writes about transformation and healing, but also about acceptance of a homosexual orientation and the need for openness with others about this. He concludes with various suggestions about the way Christians can respond individually and corporately to those who struggle with homosexuality.

Peter Saunders, who is a medical practitioner and general secretary of the Christian Medical Fellowship, contributes the final chapter, which is entitled "Nature or Nurture: The

Causes of Homosexuality." This chapter examines the changing perceptions of the medical profession regarding homosexual orientation and behavior and offers some perspectives on the limitations of scientific research. Peter then provides a helpful overview of the "nature" and "nurture" arguments for the genesis of homosexuality. Peter Saunders evaluates the debate taking place amongst researchers and warns about the misuse of their hypotheses and findings.

The majority of writers in the field of medicine and science concede that many factors are involved. Hereditary and environment are both important, and personal choice is clearly involved too. Peter concludes the chapter with a brief comment on an interactive model, to highlight the complexity and multifactorial nature of the situation. It is refreshing to read his professional assessment of the medical literature, evaluated from a self-consciously Christian critical standpoint.

The contributors to this volume want to help readers reconsider and integrate in their own thinking the biblical, theological, and medical evidence relevant to this topic. However, our concern is not simply academic, but also pastoral. We want to challenge one another to holiness of life, as defined by God himself in the pages of Scripture. We want to promote a better understanding of the nature, power, and diversity of sexual sin, refusing to allow homosexuality to be isolated from other distorted expressions of sexuality. With the call to holiness, we also want the comfort and hope of the gospel to be heard by all who struggle to be faithful in this aspect of their lives.

As this text has been prepared for a global English-speaking audience, American spelling and punctuation have been employed throughout.

*David Peterson*
*Principal of Oak Hill College*

# List of Abbreviations

| | |
|---|---|
| *AThR* | *Anglican Theological Review* |
| BAGD | Bauer, W., W. F. Arndt, and F. W. Gingrich, and F. W. Danker. *Greek-English Lexicon of the New Testament and other Early Christian Literature*. 2nd ed. Chicago: University of Chicago Press, 1979. |
| BNTC | Black's New Testament Commentaries |
| ESV | English Standard Version |
| *ExpTim* | *Expository Times* |
| Grimm-Thayer | Thayer, J. H. *A Greek-English Lexicon of the New Testament, Being Grimm's Wilke's Clavis Novi Testamenti, Translated and Enlarged*. 4th edn. Edinburgh: T. & T. Clark, 1896. |
| ICC | International Critical Commentary |
| LXX | Septuagint (Greek Version of the Old Testament) |
| *NETR* | *Near East School of Theology Theological Review* |
| NICNT | New International Commentary on the New Testament |
| NICOT | New International Commentary on the Old Testament |

| | |
|---|---|
| *NIDNTT* | *New International Dictionary of New Testament Theology*. Edited by C. Brown. 3 vols. Exeter: Paternoster, 1975-8. |
| *NIDOTTE* | *New International Dictionary of Old Testament Theology and Exegesis*. Edited by W. A. VanGemeren. 5 vols. Carlisle: Paternoster, 1997. |
| NIGTC | New International Greek Testament Commentary |
| NIV | New International Version |
| *NovT* | *Novum Testamentum* |
| NRSV | New Revised Standard Version |
| NSBT | New Studies in Biblical Theology |
| *NTS* | *New Testament Studies* |
| SNTSMS | Society for New Testament Studies Monograph Series |
| *TDNT* | *Theological Dictionary of the New Testament*. Edited by G. Kittel and G. Friedrich. 10 vols. Grand Rapids: Eerdmans, 1964-6. |
| *VC* | *Vigiliae christianae* |
| WBC | Word Biblical Commentary |

# 1

# Holiness and God's Creation Purpose

## David Peterson

> To allow the legitimacy of homosexual acts would frustrate the
> divine purpose and deny the perfection of God's provision of
> two sexes to support and complement one another.[3]

## Two starting points

### Holiness and sexuality

We live in a culture that has abandoned traditional sexual
values, many of which were informed by Scripture. Even
church leaders regularly endorse cultural, rather than scriptural, standards. When we engage in debates about sexuality,
we find ourselves confronted with fundamental questions
about the authority and sufficiency of Scripture. We are challenged to explain why the Bible's teaching on sexuality has
any relevance to our world today.

This book focuses on homosexuality because it is currently so contentious in Christian circles. Theologically and

pastorally, however, homosexuality cannot be considered in isolation from human sexual behavior more generally. What we conclude with regard to homosexuality has profound implications for what we say about every other form of sexuality. Similarly, biblical teaching about homosexuality must be understood in relation to the broader perspectives of Scripture on sexuality. One of the most serious errors in the current debate is the isolation of homosexuality from this wider context.

The following three arguments for endorsing homosexual behavior are often heard:[4]

*The "love-tolerance-unity" argument.* Love, tolerance, and unity demand the affirmation of consensual, loving same-sex erotic unions, regardless of what some Scripture texts espouse on same-sex intercourse.

*The "non-essential issue" argument.* One can find a rejection of same-sex intercourse in Scripture, but it is not a core issue and does not address the phenomenon of loving homosexual relationships.

*The "new knowledge" argument.* We have acquired medical and psychological insights that the biblical authors did not have, which renders their viewpoint obsolete.

A fourth argument has now emerged, associated particularly with Rowan Williams, the archbishop of Canterbury.[5] Homosexual practice cannot be ruled out on the basis of its non-reproductive character. Proponents of this view use the Bible to make the point that in authentic sexual encounters, our bodies become a source of happiness to ourselves and of grace to other people. The unitive aspect of sexual relations becomes the key; the self-giving desire of God as Trinity becomes the model. On this basis, committed homosexual behavior is justified and the door appears to be open for any kind of desire-based, self-giving sexual union.

In addition to such arguments, many pro-gay church leaders also bring the issue of justice for homosexuals into the discussion. But the language of holiness is rarely heard. This is remarkable since holiness is the theological context and motivation for the teaching of the Mosaic law about sexual behavior (Lev. 18:1–30; 20:7–26). Holiness is similarly the basis of Paul's appeal for distinctive sexual behavior in several key passages (e.g., 1 Thess. 4:1–8; 1 Cor. 6:9–20; 2 Cor. 6:14 – 7:2). How law and gospel differ in this connection remains to be explored. However, in terms of biblical theology, it is holiness – rather than justice, love, tolerance, unity, or personal fulfillment – that should be our first consideration.[6] Holiness is a gospel issue that cannot be sidestepped.

## The consistency of Scripture

This chapter and the next will consider the relevant biblical material on holiness and sexuality in order to demonstrate the overall consistency of Scripture on this subject. Beginning with the law of Moses, we will expose the framework and purpose of the teaching in Leviticus about sexuality. This study will enable us to see links with the fundamental purposes of God in creation, as revealed in the early chapters of Genesis. We will then turn to the teaching of Jesus, to see how he similarly highlights the foundational purposes of God in creation when considering issues of marriage and sexuality. Jesus endorses the essential teaching of the law in this area, while proclaiming the radical holiness that is at the heart of the new covenant he inaugurates.

When we study the letters of Paul against this background, it becomes clear that he, too, bases his thinking about sexual matters on the foundational purposes of God in creation. At the same time, he makes a clear connection between holiness and sexuality, as does the Mosaic law. However, the newness of the situation is that sanctification is achieved for us through the redemptive work of Christ. The outcome of that redemption is the present work of the Spirit, empowering God's people for holiness, and ultimately for the resurrection of the body. All of this is the context for the apostle's teaching about the way we use our bodies now.

# Holiness and sexuality in the law of Moses

It is often argued that it is illegitimate to use passages from Leviticus to argue the case against homosexual practice. Christians are not bound by the Mosaic law, and it seems arbitrary to hold to one set of regulations from the Torah and not to others. However, the Mosaic covenant establishes a pattern of sanctification for Israel that foreshadows the definitive work of Christ and the operation of the Holy Spirit for believers under the new covenant. Within that pattern, laws about sexual behavior and interpersonal relationships have a special place. To put it another way, there seems to be a continuity in biblical teaching about holiness and sexuality, despite the fact that both Testaments present this teaching with different emphases.

## Israel's sanctification

Under the Sinai covenant, God set Israel apart to be his own "treasured possession out of all the peoples," "a priestly kingdom and a holy nation" (Exod. 19:5–6; cf. Deut. 14:2). Holiness was a *status* conferred by divine promise and divine redemption. It was also a *calling* to be lived out in obedience to God's voice and in keeping the covenant he had made with them. A common factor in the terms describing Israel's vocation in Exodus 19:5–6 is the note of *separation* from the nations. Israel was to be uniquely at God's disposal. As "a holy nation," they were to demonstrate what it means to live under the direct rule of God, with God's sanctifying presence in their midst. As "a priestly kingdom," they were to serve the Lord exclusively and thus be a people through whom his character and will might be displayed to the world. In this way, God's original promise to bring blessing to all the nations would be enacted (see Gen. 12:1–3).[7]

It is important to dwell on this last point. Israel's sanctification was meant to be for the blessing of the nations. As Israel fulfilled her holy calling through obedience to the law, she would demonstrate to the whole world the attractiveness of being in a relationship with the one true God. God's creation purposes, marred and obscured because of sin, would be enacted and thus made clear to all. But the rest of the Old Testament shows how Israel compromised her calling and adopted the beliefs and practices of the nations. Judgement, rather than blessing and salvation, was the consequence of their lack of holiness.

Under the Sinai covenant, Israel was to avoid pollution and sin in every aspect of life and to completely break with every form of idolatry and false religion. Separation from the nations and consecration to God were two different facets of their exclusive relationship with the Lord.

## Sexuality and the covenant in the book of Leviticus

### Leviticus 1 – 16

The first sixteen chapters of Leviticus deal with laws of sacrifice, the institution of the priesthood, and various regulations about uncleanness and its treatment. By preserving Israel's purity, these cultic provisions would enable her "to remain in contact with God and witness to his presence in the world."[8] The New Testament points to the fulfillment and replacement of this tabernacle or temple cult in the person and work of the Lord Jesus Christ (e.g., Heb. 9:1 – 10:18). Under the new covenant, definitive cleansing and sanctification is available for Jews and Gentiles alike through the once-for-all sacrifice of Christ (1 Cor. 1:2, 30; 6:11).

Continual access to God "with a true heart in full assurance of faith" is possible because of the high-priestly ministry of Jesus, the exalted Messiah (Heb. 10:19–22).

### Leviticus 18 and practical holiness

Leviticus 17 – 27 offer various prescriptions for practical holiness, covering every area of Israelite life. Chapter 17 gives basic principles about food and sacrifice, chapter 18 deals specifically with sexual behavior, and chapter 19 articulates what it means to be a good neighbor, including the famous injunction to "love your neighbor as yourself" (v. 18). The list of capital and other grave crimes in Leviticus 20 covers religious and sexual behavior, showing again how family and sexual matters were central to the Old Testament view of holiness.

Leviticus 18 warns the Israelites seven times not to behave like the nations who occupied Canaan before them (vv. 3 [twice], 24, 26, 27, 29, 30). The fundamental reason for this is simply stated: "I am the LORD (your God)" (vv. 2, 4, 5, 6, 21, 30). This phrase recalls the revelation of the name of God to Israel, associated with the promise of redemption from Egypt and settlement in the promised land (Exod. 3:13–17; 6:2–9; Lev. 19:34, 36; 23:43; 25:38, 55; 26:13, 45; Num. 15:41). In Leviticus this divine self-revelation is regularly linked with the general command to be holy, because the Lord himself is holy (Lev. 11:44–45; 19:2; 20:7–8, 26). The phrase is also linked with specific instructions to indicate that "the people of God were expected to keep the law, not merely as a formal duty but as a loving response to God's grace in redemption."[9]

Negatively, therefore, there is a continuing challenge in Leviticus 18 to turn away from the practices of the nations, including incestuous relationships (vv. 6–18), adultery (v. 20), offering children in sacrifice (v. 21), homosexual behavior (v. 22), and bestiality (v. 23). Positively, there is the continuing challenge to be different because of who God is (vv. 2–4) and because his rules offer true life (v. 5, cf. 26:3–13), rather than uncleanness, which leads to judgement (vv. 24–30).

### Homosexuality in this context

Homosexuality is described as "an abomination" (Lev. 18:22, cf. 20:13; Heb. *tôʿēbâ*), meaning something abhorred or hated. The implication is that certain practices are hated by God and should therefore be hated by his people. In Leviticus 18:26, 27, 29, and 30, the term is employed to describe everything prohibited in the chapter. In biblical usage, it does not simply speak of idolatry, as some have argued, nor does it limit the prohibition against homosexuality to cult prostitution.[10]

Leviticus 18:22 and 20:13 both use the general term "male" (Heb. *zākār,* as in Gen. 1:27), thus forbidding every kind of male-male intercourse. Leviticus 20:13 condemns both partners equally. Furthermore, both texts use the term "lie with" (Heb. *škb* with a preposition), rather than a verb which may suggest rape or any kind of forced relationship.[11] The phrase "as with a woman" indicates that what is condemned is sexual activity in which a male puts another male in the position of a female. In short, these texts condemn homosexual intercourse where both parties consent, whether it is practiced privately or in connection with pagan worship.

Gordon Wenham explains the distinctiveness of these prohibitions in the light of what can be known about attitudes towards homosexuality among Israel's neighbors:

> The ancient Near East was a world in which the practice of homosexuality was well known. It was an integral part of temple life at least in parts of Mesopotamia, and no blame appears to have attached to its practice outside of worship. Those who regularly played the passive role in intercourse were despised for being effeminate, and certain relationships such as father-son or pederasty were regarded as wrong, but otherwise it was regarded as quite respectable.[12]

Set against this background, the Old Testament laws are very striking. These laws ban every type of homosexual activity – not just forcible intercourse as the Assyrians did, or sex with youths as the Egyptians did.

### Reflecting the perspectives of Genesis

This distinctiveness cannot simply be explained in terms of Israel's aversion to the customs of her neighbors. The opening chapters of Genesis express many of the most fundamental principles of Old Testament theology. The biblical view of creation is that God created the different plants and animals to reproduce according to their own particular type. "Hence the law forbids any mixed breeding or acts that might encourage it (Lev. 19:19; Deut. 22:5, 9–11)."[13] Genesis speaks of the creation of humankind in two sexes, in order to "be fruitful and multiply" (1:28), but also so that male and female might relate together in total intimacy and become "one flesh" (2:18–24). Wenham concludes:

> It therefore seems most likely that Israel's repudiation of homosexual intercourse arises out of its doctrine of creation . . . To allow the legitimacy of homosexual acts would frustrate the divine purpose and deny the perfection of God's provision of two sexes to support and complement one another.[14]

More generally, Mary Douglas makes the same point. Holiness means keeping the categories of creation distinct:

> It therefore involves correct definition, discrimination and order. Under this head all the rules of sexual morality exemplify the holy. Incest and adultery (Lev. 18:6–20) are against holiness, in the simple sense of right order. Morality does not conflict with holiness, but holiness is more a matter of separating that which should be separated than of protecting the rights of husbands and brothers.[15]

The Apostle Paul seems to reflect this view of creation when he describes homosexual behavior as "unnatural" (Gk. *para physin*, Rom. 1:26). We will explore this issue further in chapter 3. Sanctification under old and new covenants involves *God's enabling of his people to live according to the "right order" that he has established for relationships* (1 Cor. 6:9–11). This will be explored in Chapter 2.

## Sexuality and the death penalty

### Leviticus 20 in context

The laws in Leviticus 20 appear in casuistic form, stating the consequences for breaking prohibitions such as those in Leviticus 18. The chapter begins with the penalty for idolatry and seeking after mediums and wizards (vv. 1–6). A call to holiness (vv. 7–8) precedes the central section dealing with family life (vv. 9–21). A second call to holiness (vv. 22–26) leads to a final statement about the penalty for being a medium or wizard (v. 27).

These exhortations to holiness and the warnings about transgressors being "cut off" from among the people (vv. 3, 5, 6, 17, 18) make it clear that the provisions are specifically for national Israel. They were living in the land that God had given them, and they were not to pollute themselves and their inheritance with the practices of the nations (vv. 22–26). Having been separated from those nations to belong to God, they were to maintain the separation by removing everything from their midst that offended God. The death penalty was an indication of the seriousness of this call to holiness.

The ultimate ground for the death penalty in Scripture lies in the creation and fall narratives of Genesis. God threatens death (2:17) and imposes it (3:19) as his response to human rebellion. The sentence is universal, and God himself puts it into effect. After the flood, however, God gives human judges a limited responsibility in this area (9:6). Murder is identified as a capital offense "because it is a direct assault on the created order established by God, in which man, made in his image, functions as his representative."[16] The penalties of the Mosaic law must also be read against the background of Genesis 1 – 3:

> The Sinai Covenant must be seen as a particular expression of the relationship between God and the world implicit in creation itself, and incest, adultery and homosexuality as violations of the created order.[17]

## Capital crimes in Leviticus 20

Capital crimes listed at the heart of Leviticus 20 include the cursing of parents (v. 9) rather than honoring them as the Decalogue commands, adultery (v. 10), incest with close relatives (vv. 11, 12, 14), homosexual activity (v. 13), and bestiality (vv. 15–16). Wenham notes three main types of punishment in the Pentateuch: the death penalty for the gravest public sins against life, religion, and the family; "cutting off" for grave private sins; and restitution for property sins.[18] Religious offenses, as well as offenses against life and the structure of the family, tended to be punished more severely in Israel than elsewhere in the ancient Near East.

Once again, we must note that the theology of holiness is fundamental to these laws. It is necessary to exclude from the holy community of Israel those people and practices that deny God's purpose for his creation and ignore the consequences of disobedience. In this way, the integrity of the holy community is protected so that its witness to the world can be maintained. The death penalty thus relates to the particular circumstances of historic Israel, as a community formed to manifest God's holiness in all its dimensions to a fallen world. Since holiness and sexuality are linked under the new covenant, we will need to consider what penalty the writers of the New Testament envisage in connection with persistent unholy behavior.

# The New Testament and the law of Moses

As we begin to consider the relevance of the Levitical material for contemporary debates about sexuality, we need to ask more fundamental questions about the role of the Mosaic law in the life of Christians. We can make only a few brief comments on this subject here. Chapter 2 will offer a more detailed analysis of the way in which the Apostle Paul uses the teaching of the law in connection with his reflections on sexual matters. Clearly, however, the perspective of Jesus on the law, and more specifically on sexuality, is of great significance.

## Jesus and the law

Jesus' attitude to the law is a complex and much discussed issue. He takes the sacrificial system and the associated cult as a given (e.g., Matt. 5:23–24; Mark 1:44; 12:41–44), but he often stands with the Old Testament prophets in condemning the cultic practices and traditions of his contemporaries. At the same time, Jesus claims to "fulfill" the law (Matt. 5:17), most obviously in his teaching, but also apparently in his living, and in his dying.[19] His ministry is a transitional stage in salvation history, in which he prepares his disciples for a new era.

## Written on the heart

In the Sermon on the Mount, Matthew shows how "the law finds its prophetic centre in Jesus but not necessarily its end."[20] Jesus goes beyond the wooden literalism of his own day and makes a radical demand for the interiorization of the law. In this way, he points to the inauguration of the new covenant promised in Jeremiah 31:31–34. There God indicates his intention to put his law "within" his people and to "write it on their hearts." This does not imply the abandonment of the law's teaching. Together with the amazing provision of a definitive forgiveness of sins, God will help his faithless people to know his will better and to be personally renewed in their commitment to him (Ezek. 36:25–27).

A challenge about sexual purity and faithfulness in marriage stands at the center of Jesus' prophetic application of the law to the messianic community (Matt. 5:27–32). He warns that lust, being adultery in the heart, is sufficient to condemn the unrepentant to the judgement of hell. Divorce under certain circumstances may cause someone to commit adultery. A call to "be perfect, as your heavenly Father is perfect" (5:48) concludes the first section of the Sermon on the Mount and recalls the Levitical challenge, "You shall be holy, for I the LORD your God am holy" (Lev. 19:2). Those living in a new covenant relationship with God must, fundamentally, reflect God's character, and it is Jesus himself who establishes the parameters of that relationship.

## Dealing with defilement

The Pharisees and scribes complained that Jesus' disciples defiled themselves by not observing "the tradition of the elders" about ritual washing before taking food (Mark 7:1–5; Matt. 15:1–2). In a subsequent address to the crowds, Jesus raises the issue of the true source of defilement (Mark 7:15; Matt. 15:11). His teaching does not directly attack Old Testament laws about ritual cleanness. "It moves in a different realm altogether, for it expresses an entirely new understanding of what does and does not constitute defilement."[21] True purity before God cannot be obtained by scrupulous observance of cultic laws because rituals are unable to deal with the defilement that comes from within, from a rebellious and corrupt "heart" (Mark 7:17–23; Matt. 15:16–20; recalling Isa. 29:13).

In this context, Jesus uses a range of terms to describe unacceptable sexual behavior (Mark 7:20–23). Sexual immorality (Gk. *porneiai*, a general term), adultery (*moicheiai,* a specific term) and sensuality (*aselgeia,* a general term for sexual excesses or licentiousness) are listed with many other things that "come from within" and "defile a person." Although Jesus does not refer explicitly to same-sex intercourse, "no first-century Jew could have spoken of *porneiai* (plural) without having in mind the list of forbidden sexual offenses in Leviticus 18 and 20 (incest, adultery, same-sex intercourse, bestiality)."[22]

The prescriptions of the Mosaic covenant for ritual cleansing were a sign of the need for purification in a more profound and complete sense. Jesus' teaching raises a question about where such cleansing might be found. The immediate context provides no answer, although his teaching about the significance of his death ultimately offers the solution to this problem. He will give his life as "a ransom for many" (Matt. 20:28; Mark 10:45) and will thus inaugurate the new covenant, which promises a definitive forgiveness of sins (Matt. 26:28; Luke 22:20; cf. Jer. 31:34).

### Continuity and discontinuity

Mark's editorial note on the discourse about ritual uncleanness draws out the implications of Jesus' teaching for the benefit of his readers ("thus he declared all foods clean," 7:19). Mark indicates that the food laws are not binding on those to whom his Gospel is addressed. This teaching anticipates the vision given to Peter in Acts 10:9–16, with its assurance that the purity laws of the Mosaic covenant are not applicable under the new covenant. The holiness of God's people is no longer to be defined in such terms, but holiness is still to be expressed in moral terms (e.g., 1 Thess. 4:1–8; 1 Pet. 1:13–16).

Jesus' teaching about marriage and divorce (Matt. 19:2–12; Mark 10:2–12) points to a specific continuity between Old and New Testaments in this connection.

Although he does not use the terminology of holiness here, he clearly shows that God's demand for sexual purity remains as exacting as ever for those who are his children. Pointing to Genesis 2:24 as normative, Jesus confirms that "the Mosaic legislation was intended, in general, to reflect the created order as represented in Genesis 2 and to prevent violations of it. Jesus' teaching gives fresh expression to this basic principle."[23] He recognizes only marriage between a man and a woman as the proper context for sexual union.

Far from loosing the moral demands of the law, Jesus seems to be at pains to point out the deeper implications of God's revelation to Israel (Matt. 5:17–20). He does this by way of example in the Sermon on the Mount and elsewhere – not by an exhaustive comment on every aspect of the Levitical teaching on sexuality.

Although Jesus does not address the question of homosexuality directly, his response to the disciples' challenge ("If such is the case of a man with his wife, it is better not to marry," Matt. 19:10) is relevant to the debate. He indicates that some may be impotent, some may have been castrated, and some may make a voluntary decision to make themselves eunuchs, "for the sake of the kingdom of heaven" (19:11–12). His call is for abstinent singleness here. "Christ's coming and the inbreaking of God's kingdom opens up a new way of life which, without denying the goodness of marriage, forgoes marriage for the sake of the kingdom (Matt. 19:11–12; 1 Cor. 7)."[24]

"The portrayal of Jesus as a first-century Palestinian Jew who was open to homosexual practice is simply ahistorical. All the evidence leads in the opposite direction."[25] His calling is to faithful heterosexual marriage and abstinent singleness. With regard to the latter, the example of his own life is "of vital importance in shaping the Christian vision of sexual behaviour."[26]

## Some Pauline perspectives

Paul's teaching about the law is also complex and much
debated. Chapter 2 gives particular attention to his teaching
regarding holiness and sexuality. At this point, I would simply draw attention to two foundational notions in his letters.
First, there is the principle of freedom from the law. As
Christians we are released from the law's penalties and the
law's dominion, so that we may belong to the risen Christ
and "bear fruit for God" (Rom. 7:4). Now we serve God "not
under the old written code but in the new life of the Spirit"
(Rom. 7:6). But secondly, there is also the principle of reap-
plication in Christ. "Whatever was written in former days
was written for our instruction, so that by steadfastness and
by the encouragement of the scriptures we might have hope"
(Rom. 15:4).

Every part of what we call the Old Testament has something to teach us about God's purposes for humanity and the
whole created order. The plan of salvation through Christ is
revealed there, and the pattern of holiness revealed to Israel
prepares for the pattern revealed by Christ (2 Cor. 6:14 – 7:1).
The holiness of God's people is supposed to bear witness to
the world concerning God's character and intentions.
Moreover, Scripture is not intended to depress us and defeat
us but to give us hope, as we understand the way it is fulfilled
in Christ. We need, therefore, to reflect on the way in which
Paul's teaching on sexuality and holiness is constrained and
directed by the Old Testament.

## The call to holiness in 1 Peter

As a parallel to Paul's teaching, it is interesting to observe
briefly the way in which 1 Peter reflects the broad perspectives
of the Mosaic law. In the law, we discern the principles of
holiness by which the people of God were to be distinguished

from the world and its values. But we have already noted that the call to holiness was designed to bring blessing to the world, enabling God's people to bear witness to the Creator and his purposes. In 1 Peter, there is an explicit challenge to "be holy yourselves in all your conduct" (1:15–16, cf. Lev. 11:44–45) and a declaration that "holy nation" status now belongs to the disciples of Christ (2:9–10, alluding to Exod. 19:5–6). Following this are exhortations to behave before the world in such a way that unbelievers may "see your honorable deeds and glorify God when he comes to judge" (2:12; cf. Matt. 5:16). These exhortations include the general challenge "to abstain from the desires of the flesh that wage war against the soul" (2:11). Although Peter later gives some idea of what these passions might include (4:2–4), it is likely that he expected his readers to understand the details of what God requires for his people from the Old Testament Scriptures and the teaching of Jesus.

## Conclusion

We have examined the specific connection between laws about sexuality and the demand for holiness under the old covenant. Holiness in the Old Testament is not simply a matter of being different from the unbelieving world or protesting against the lifestyle of the unbelieving. It is first and foremost a status given by God to his people, and then a demand to live out the relationship made possible by God's gracious provision. The challenge is to reflect God's character and purposes in a positive way, demonstrating his will for humanity and the created order. Since marriage and sexuality are fundamental to our existence as men and women, it is not surprising that we see strong links between the provisions of Leviticus and the teaching of Genesis 1 – 3. The Levitical laws define the way in which

God's intentions for marriage and sexuality are to be guarded and expressed.

The priesthood and sacrificial ritual of the book of Leviticus have been fulfilled and replaced for us by the person and work of the Lord Jesus Christ. Furthermore, the New Testament speaks about the people of Christ being sanctified by his redemptive work. Holiness is no longer to be expressed in terms of food or ritual. But the New Testament continues to link holiness with the demand for sexual purity and loving relationships. Jesus' own teaching in this area shows the continuity of God's demand. He grounds his prescriptions in Genesis and draws out the implications of the Mosaic law in this area. The Apostle Paul develops this biblical theological trajectory in ways which we must now examine in some detail.

As Christians, we are not "under the law" as Israel was. But Jesus and Paul, his apostle, make it clear that the teaching of the law about marriage and sexuality cannot be ignored or set aside. The moral provisions of the law must be understood and applied in terms of scriptural revelation as a whole. Their relational dimension makes them fundamental to God's creative and redemptive purposes.

# 2

# Holiness and Sexuality in the Pauline Writings

## David Peterson

> Dividing doctrine from ethics not only creates the possibility for serious mistakes in Christian thinking but also diminishes the coherence of the life of holiness which is the Christian vocation.[27]

The demand for holiness which is central to Leviticus and the whole Mosaic law (e.g., Exod. 19:6; Lev. 19:2; 20:7; 21:8) remains at the heart of Christian exhortation in the New Testament (e.g., Col. 3:12–17; 1 Thess. 4:1–8; Heb. 12:14; 1 Pet. 1:13–16). The apostolic writings reinterpret and apply a number of fundamental prohibitions and exhortations found in the Mosaic law, to tease out for us what it means to be God's holy people under the new covenant. The essential theological point is that Christians are to be distinct from the world in values and behavior, because they belong to the Lord Jesus Christ. Holiness is a gospel issue because Christ's redemptive work makes a new form of sanctification possible. Holiness of life is a sign of true conversion and allegiance to Christ. Failure to pursue holiness indicates a life out of touch with the Lord and his will.

# Abstaining from sexual immorality
# (1 Thess. 4:1–8)

### *The will of God for Christians*

In his first letter to the Thessalonians, Paul reminds his converts that they had received instructions from him "through the Lord Jesus" on how they ought to live and to please God (1 Thess. 4:1–2). He urges them to follow these instructions more and more and declares that the will of God for them is their "sanctification."[28] Holiness of life under the new covenant flows from consecration to God in Christ (1 Cor. 1:2, 30; 6:11; Eph. 5:26–27; 2 Thess. 2:13). The immediate context indicates that this holiness involves obedience to apostolic teaching, which comes with the authority of the Lord Jesus himself. In particular, Paul declares that holiness involves abstaining from all forms of *porneia* (1 Thess. 4:3).

Paul appears to mean by *porneia* any form of sexual relationship outside marriage.[29] The challenge is amplified in these terms: "that each one of you knows how to control your own body in holiness and honor, not with lustful passion, like the Gentiles who do not know God" (vv. 4–5).[30] Those who have come to know God in Jesus Christ will treat their bodies as *his* property. If our bodies belong to the Lord, we are no longer free to use them selfishly or according to the accepted values of the time.

There are two basic principles here, which Paul later develops in 1 Corinthians. First, the body, which has been redeemed "for the Lord," and which is now "a temple of the Holy Spirit," cannot be used in a way that is contrary to God's revealed will (1 Cor. 6:13–20). So believers are to "flee from sexual immorality" (1 Cor. 6:18, *porneia*). Second, when God gives the gift of marriage to a man and a woman, their bodies belong to one another. Husbands and wives should use their bodies exclusively for the benefit and pleasure of their spouse (1 Cor. 7:3–4). In these passages, the notion of "belonging," which is fundamental to the concept of holiness, is shown to be the basis of Paul's sexual ethic. Belonging to God involves belonging to one another within the boundaries that God defines.

Some have argued that Paul introduces a new subject in 1 Thessalonians 4:6, warning against the exploitation of a "brother" in the field of commerce.[31] It is certainly critical to see God's call for holiness extending to every sphere of life, but there are no compelling reasons to conclude that Paul moves away from his focus on sexual matters in this verse. Indeed, the mention of "impurity" or "uncleanness" (Gk. *akatharsia*) in verse 7 confirms that the subject of the preceding verse is sexual rather than commercial behavior. Christians must beware of trespassing against brothers and sisters in Christ by behaving covetously (v. 6, Gk. *pleonektein*). Honoring God with our bodies also means being careful not to injure others by our behavior. By crossing forbidden sexual boundaries, we risk harming not only ourselves but others as well. Here Paul may have in mind the sort of boundaries set out in the Levitical law, where holiness and sexual behavior are closely linked. The Lord Jesus himself is "an avenger in all these things" and will inflict the appropriate judgement on those who disregard his will (v. 6b; cf. 2 Thess. 1:6–10).

The flow of the argument in verses 6–7 suggests that the coming judgement and God's initial calling of us "in holiness" are to be the ground and motivation for distinctive Christian living. God did not call us "for impurity." Rather, by setting us apart for himself, he indicated his desire for us to live differently, as those who belong to him. Those who know that they are loved and possessed by God experience the strength to live differently.

## *The gift of the Spirit*

1 Thessalonians 4:8 introduces a final reason for obeying God in sexual matters with the emphatic connecting word "therefore" (Gk. *toigaroun*). "Therefore whoever rejects this rejects not human authority but God, who also gives his Holy Spirit to you." Paul returns here to the point made in verses 1–2, insisting that his instructions come with divine authority. Those who teach a more permissive policy or disregard Paul's words by their actions are setting aside the explicit will of God. Indeed, the Spirit God gives to Christians is the Spirit of *holiness,* and nothing unholy can be tolerated in the lives of individuals or communities where the Holy Spirit dwells (1 Cor. 3:16–17; 6:19–20; 2 Cor. 6:14 – 7:1). As Paul puts it elsewhere, the Spirit is given to make it possible for God's people to exhibit the fruit of "love, joy, peace, patience, kindness, generosity, faithfulness, gentleness, and self-control" (Gal. 5:22–23).

Paul grounds his exhortation to holiness in 1 Thessalonians 4:8 by appealing to the fact of *God's continuous, sanctifying presence.*[32] His reference to God giving the Spirit specifically recalls the promise of Ezekiel 36:27 ("I will put my spirit within you, and make you follow my statutes and be careful to observe my ordinances"). Moving to a related theme in verse 9, Paul says, "now concerning love of the brothers and sisters, you do not need to have anyone write to you, for you yourselves have been taught by God to love one another." He notes how they have generously expressed their love, but he urges them "to do so more and more" (v. 10). Here, the ground of his appeal is the fact that they have been "taught by God," which is a way of proclaiming the fulfillment of Jeremiah 31:34 ("No longer shall they teach one another, or say to each other, 'Know the LORD,' for they shall all know me, from the least of them to the greatest").[33]

God is at work in the people of the new covenant through the energizing and consecrating power of his Spirit (1 Thess. 4:8), teaching and molding them through his implanted word to conform to his will (v. 9). Reflecting on the law of God and its implications in the light of Christ's coming will be an aspect of this teaching and molding. Both verses imply that "it is God's activity within the hearts of Christians that *impels* them to action."[34] God's holiness – what he essentially is – is present to us in the Holy Spirit. God's Spirit demands and makes possible the reflection of his holiness in the lives of his people. We must not resist his Spirit by unchaste or loveless behavior, but rather "abound" in love (v. 10), which effectively means abounding in holiness (4:1; 3:11–13).

## Purging the church of sexual immorality (1 Cor. 5:1–13)

In 1 Corinthians 5:1 – 6:20, Paul demonstrates that "certain moral principles stand above and beyond situational variables."[35] He first confronts a particular case of sexual immorality and condemns the complacency and arrogance of the church about this evil in their midst (5:1–13). We see here that the general term *porneia* (5:1; cf. 1 Thess. 4:3) also includes an incestuous relationship. In Deuteronomy 27:20 such behavior stands under the curse of God, which in Leviticus 20:11 means the death penalty. What penalty does the New Testament apply in such a situation?

The apostolic injunction is to remove such a person from the church (1 Cor. 5:2). This punishment is further described as cleaning out "the yeast of malice and evil" (5:7–8) and driving the wicked person from their midst (5:13). Such discipline is clearly designed to preserve the holiness of the church, even though this terminology is not specifically used. Paul makes it clear that he is not telling Christians to cut themselves off from "the [sexually] immoral of this world, or the greedy and robbers, or idolaters, since you would then need to go out of the world" (5:10). Rather, his concern is that believers should not "associate with anyone who bears the name of brother or sister who is sexually immoral or greedy, or is an idolater, reviler, drunkard, or robber." Indeed, he says, "Do not even eat with such a one" (5:11).

Sudden removal of an unrepentant offender from the believing community is also described as delivering or handing him over "to Satan for the destruction of the flesh, so that his spirit may be saved in the day of the Lord" (5:5). Such a move is designed to purge the person and the church of "its fleshly stance of self-sufficiency."[36] Removed from the sphere of God's protection within the church and exposed to the satanic forces of evil in the world, the hope is that the offender will repent and so be saved and not finally lost. Paul later insists that those who persist in such behavior without repentance "will not inherit the kingdom of God" (6:9–10).

In our tolerant and complacent age, it is hard for Christians to take such warnings and injunctions seriously. We may readily agree with Paul that we should not judge outsiders, since that is God's responsibility (5:12–13). But we find it extremely difficult to accept the message that we are to judge those inside the church. We can only grasp the importance of this command and obey it appropriately when we have recovered a sense of the holiness of God and of God's concern to manifest his holiness in the lives of his people.

## The power to change (1 Cor. 6:9–11)

### *The lifestyle of the ungodly*

In 1 Corinthians 6:9–10 Paul makes it clear that the unrighteous "will not inherit the kingdom of God." He has already used the term "unrighteous" (v. 1) to describe "unbelievers" (v. 6), in contrast with "the saints" who will "judge the world" (vv. 1–2). The "saints" are those who have been washed, sanctified, and justified "in the name of the Lord Jesus Christ and in the Spirit of our God" (v. 11; cf. 1 Cor. 1:2). The unrighteous are those whose lives have not yet been transformed by the Lord and his Spirit.

Those who will not inherit the kingdom of God are further described as the sexually immoral, idolaters, adulterers, the passive and active partners in consenting homosexual acts, thieves, the greedy, drunkards, revilers, and robbers (vv. 9–10). This is not a comprehensive list, but it shows that there is a distinct pattern of behavior that characterizes "the unrighteous" and differentiates them from "the saints."

The list in 6:9–10 adds six categories of sin to the four already listed in 5:10–11. Sexual immorality in all its forms is included with idolatry, dishonesty, greed, and various expressions of self-indulgence and disorderliness. Each item is regarded as being equally serious in God's eyes. None is worse than any other. Some of the Corinthians appear to have been practicing these vices.[37] They are warned to "stop deceiving themselves" or to "not be deceived." If they persist in such behavior, they show themselves to be unconverted. A different lifestyle is appropriate for those who are "sanctified in Christ Jesus" (1:2; 6:11).

Some scholars have argued that Paul is developing a catalogue of vices that reflects little more than the culture-relative conventions of his day. He simply writes from the perspective of a Greco-Roman moralist. However, Anthony Thiselton shows that all of the terms in Paul's list have an Old Testament background, and that the theological and ethical framework of the apostle's appeal is distinctly biblical. "Christian corporate identity has a distinctive foundation and a distinctive lifestyle as against Graeco-Roman social, political and religious traditions."[38]

## The behavior to be rejected

The "sexually immoral" (Gk. *pornoi*, cf. *porneia* in 1 Thess. 4:3) will include those who engage in incestuous behavior (5:1) and prostitution (6:13, 18, because the word *pornē* is used in v. 16). "Adulterers" more specifically refers to married persons engaging in sexual relationships of any kind outside marriage. Paul adds two new terms in 6:9 (Gk. *malakoi, arsenokoitai*), to bring consenting homosexuality into the frame.

There has been great debate regarding the meaning of these two words. The adjective "soft" (*malakos*) was used in the Greco-Roman world to describe those who were effeminate and allowed themselves to be treated as women. There was another technical term for young men who sold themselves as "mistresses" in a pederastic relationship with older men, but *malakoi* seems to refer to such passive homosexual behavior in this context because it is coupled with *arsenokoitai*.[39]

The latter term, *arsenokoitai*, appears here and in 1 Timothy 1:10 for the first time in extant Greek literature, and it is used sparingly by subsequent authors. It is a compound of "male" and "intercourse" and could simply refer to male prostitutes of any kind. John Boswell argues that it refers to "a male who engages in vulgar sexual intercourse" and denies that it refers to homosexuality at all.[40] He insists that the term could not have been derived from the language of Leviticus about homosexuality:

> It would simply not have occurred to most early Christians to invoke the authority of the old law to justify the morality of the new: the Levitical regulations had no hold on Christians and are manifestly irrelevant in explaining Christian hostility to gay sexuality.[41]

More recent scholars, however, have argued that Paul's term is indeed a translation of the Hebrew *mishkav zakur* ("lying with a male"), derived from Leviticus 18:22; 20:13, and used in Rabbinic texts to refer to homosexual intercourse.[42] It reflects closely the LXX of Leviticus 20:13 (*meta arsenos koitēn*) and could be a deliberate way of alluding to the prohibition of the Mosaic law. It literally means "bedders of males," or "men who sleep with men." It cannot legitimately be broadened to include any kind of immoral sexual behavior by males, nor can it be narrowed to exploitative same-sex intercourse.[43]

Together, *malakoi* and *arsenokoitai* appear to cover the full range of homosexual behavior – the first word having the sense of passivity in classical usage, and the second having more active connotations in Leviticus.[44] Paul did not simply take over a conventional list of vices from Hellenistic authors, whether Jewish or secular. He opposed homosexuality because "it is marked as a vice in the Torah,"[45] where it is presented as behavior inconsistent with the holiness demanded of God's people.

## Why believers are different

"This is what some of you used to be," Paul affirms. "But you were washed, you were sanctified, you were justified in the name of the Lord Jesus Christ and in the Spirit of our God" (1 Cor. 6:11). His overall meaning is this:

> Your own conversion, effected by God through the work of Christ and the Spirit, is what has removed you from being amongst the wicked, who will not inherit the kingdom . . . Therefore, live out this new life in Christ and stop being like the wicked.[46]

As in 1 Corinthians 1:30, Paul uses three metaphors here to explain how the saving work of Christ can benefit us. Each verb in the aorist passive tense in Greek is preceded by the

strong adversative "but" (Gk. *alla*), although English transla-
tions rarely make this clear. Paul is offering three different
descriptions of the same reality, rather than alluding to a
process of being washed, then sanctified, and then justified.

In the context, "you were washed" (Gk. *apelousasthe*)
implies a cleansing from the defilement of sin. It is another
way of talking about the effect of Christ's sacrifice on those
who believe the gospel. It is possible that Paul is alluding to
baptism here, in which case he will be highlighting the spiritual cleansing which is sacramentally signified in baptism
(cf. Eph. 5:26; Heb. 10:22).[47] The same verb is used in Acts
22:16, where Ananias says to Paul, "Get up, be baptized and
have your sins washed away, calling on his name."[48]

When Paul says "you were justified" (Gk. *edikaiōthēte*), he
employs the verb *dikaioun*, which comes from the same root
as the noun *dikaiosynē* ("righteousness, justification") in
1 Corinthians 1:30. The verb denotes,

> God's powerful, cosmic and universal action in effecting a
> change in the situation between sinful humanity and God, by
> which God is able to acquit and vindicate believers, setting them
> in a right and faithful relation to himself.[49]

"You were sanctified" (Gk. *hēgiasthēte*) similarly corresponds
with a noun used in 1 Corinthians 1:30 (*hagiasmos*, "holiness,
sanctification"). This terminology does not refer to a process
of ethical development but highlights the fact that God
claimed them as his own and made them members of his holy
people (cf. 1:2). He turned them around and brought them to
himself in faith and love. In ethical terms, however, such a
separation from previous attachments and values has profound implications: "because of what God has done, the possibility of a new life is open to them; they are (in the language
of v. 7) 'unleavened,' and they must now purge out the old
leaven and keep the Christian feast in sincerity and truth."[50]

Paul uses the language of conversion or Christian initia-
tion to make an implied moral appeal,

> that having been once *justified,* they must not draw down upon
> themselves a new condemnation – that having been *sanctified,*
> they must not pollute themselves anew – that, having been
> *washed,* they must not disgrace themselves with new defile-
> ments, but, on the contrary, aim at purity, persevere in true holi-
> ness, and abominate their former pollutions.[51]

This new situation is initiated and maintained from a human
point of view by trusting in the power of Christ's "name" and
by continuing to call upon that name. The Spirit is the means
whereby God "effects the work of Christ in the believer's life."[52]

## Practical implications

Our essential identity as Christians is formed by Christ and
the gospel, not by our own personalities, backgrounds, or
achievements.[53] Through the death and resurrection of his
Son, God has cleansed us from the guilt of sin and liberated
us from its consequences and its control. He has set us in a
right and faithful relation to himself, together with all who
call upon the name of our Lord Jesus Christ. Drawing us into
an exclusive relationship with himself in this way, he has
made us his holy people, destined to serve him and please
him forever. Sanctification is about being possessed by God
and expressing that distinctive and exclusive relationship by
the way we live.[54]

This is an important perspective for all of us to grasp, not
least those who struggle with homosexual temptation. The
gay community encourages people to "come out" and
acknowledge that they are homosexuals, expressing who
they are by engaging in homosexual behavior. However, the
gospel tells us that our identity is formed by Christ and what

he has done for us. We are no longer to think of ourselves as essentially idolaters or homosexuals, as drunkards or thieves, but as Christians who struggle with temptation in these or other ways. Whatever our background and past experience, in Christ we are part of the new creation he came to inaugurate: "the old has passed away; see, everything has become new!" (2 Cor. 5:17).

Those who are bowed down by the pressure of temptation or are aware of failure need to be reminded of the definitive, sanctifying work of God in Christ, by which he has established us as his holy people. On this basis, these people should be urged to press on in hope and grasp again by faith the benefits of Christ's sacrifice. As in 1 Thessalonians 4, the challenge to holiness in 1 Corinthians 6:9–11 is accompanied by a reference to the Holy Spirit, whom God has given to enable his people to pursue holiness.

## Glorifying God with your body (1 Cor. 6:12–20)

The end of 1 Corinthians 6 makes explicit the idea that the Christian's body is for the Lord, and not for self-gratification. Although verses 12–20 do not use holiness language, the emphasis on being redeemed and therefore owned by the Lord conveys a similar perspective. As does the Levitical law, this passage emphasizes that the body is a means of glorifying God, although here the believer's union with Christ and hope of resurrection give a special significance to that responsibility.

### *A false spirituality*

Paul appears to dissociate himself from three Corinthian slogans here. Firstly, "All things are lawful for me" (v. 12) implies a freedom to do anything in the sexual realm. Secondly, "'Food is meant for the stomach and the stomach for food,' and God will destroy both one and the other" (v. 13) implies that neither eating nor sexual behavior have any significance for our future destiny. Thirdly, he rejects the idea that "every sin that a person commits is outside the body" (v. 18). The apostle is not addressing "libertines" here but "spiritual" people, "who extend freedom about food offered to idols (6:12; 10:23; 8:1 – 11:1) to wider issues about 'the body.'"[55] As before, "the gospel itself is at stake, not simply the resolution of an ethical question."[56]

Paul's response to the first slogan is not to deny the principle of Christian liberty but to qualify it with the words, "but not all things are beneficial." These words anticipate his use of edification terminology in 8:1, 10; 10:23; 14:4, 17, suggesting that his concern is not simply for what helps individuals but for what helps the Christian community to express its true identity and purpose. Paul also insists that he will not be enslaved by anything, implying that unqualified freedom brings bondage.

The second slogan reveals more of the theological agenda driving the spirituality that Paul attacks. His opponents are trying to separate deeds done in the body – with regard to food or sex or property – and the spiritual life. This sort of dualism was common in the Greco-Roman world in circles influenced by "a popular form of quasi-Platonic thought."[57] It has resurfaced whenever Christians have had a weak or inadequate view of the resurrection of the body. Perhaps a misunderstanding of the teaching of Jesus about defilement (cf. Mark 7:14–23; Matt. 15:16–20) underlies this idea about food and the stomach. Did freedom from food laws mean freedom from every other restraint?

While it is true that "'Food is meant for the stomach and the stomach for food,' and God will destroy both one and the other," that is not the whole story. God raised the Lord Jesus bodily and will raise us up similarly "by his power" (v. 14; cf. 15:35–49). This is the basis for Paul's assertion that, "the body is not meant for sexual immorality, but for the Lord, and the Lord for the body" (v. 13, NIV). The change from "stomach" to "body" is significant: body is "one of several terms used by Paul to denote not one part of man's nature but man as a whole."[58] The Old Testament clearly affirms God's ownership of our bodies and his right to direct the way in which we should use them. However, it is the eschatological perspective that gives an even greater significance to this biblical teaching (Rom. 6:12–13, 17–19; 12:1; Phil. 3:17–21). God will raise us as a transformed humanity, "as the single in-Christ corporeity, for whom 'bodily' existence matters."[59]

## The Lord and the body

Paul makes the extraordinary claim that "your bodies are members of Christ" (1 Cor. 6:15). Elsewhere he calls for us to present the "members" (Gk. *melē*) of our bodies to God as "instruments of righteousness" (Rom. 6:13; cf. 6:19). He also speaks in various ways about Christians being "members" of the body of Christ (e.g., Rom. 12:4–5; 1 Cor. 12:12–14, 18–20, 25–27) and therefore "members one of another" (Eph. 4:25). However, here in 1 Corinthians 6 Paul lays the emphasis on ourselves as a totality, in our bodily existence, being "united to the Lord" (v. 17, Gk. *kollaō*). "The body of the believer is *for* the Lord because through Christ's resurrection God has set in motion the reality of our own resurrection."[60] Those who have been "bought with a price" belong to Christ in a physical way (6:19–20). Their union with Christ is more than spiritual. They cannot take back what belongs to Christ and use it for un-Christlike purposes.

The apostle uses the same verb to "join" (Gk. *kollaō*) in his warning about going to a prostitute and becoming "one body with her" (v. 16). The language here recalls the LXX of

Genesis 2:24 (where *proskollaō* is used). Paul quotes part of this text to support his argument ("For it is said, 'The two shall be one flesh'"). The union of Christians with Christ is likened to a marriage. Our bodies belong to Christ. "The man who has sex with a prostitute is, in Paul's construction, Christ's 'member' entering the body of the prostitute."[61] To take away that which belongs to Christ and join it to another is to deny God's purpose in creation and redemption. Lack of devotion to Christ contradicts the "betrothal" to Christ (2 Cor. 11:2–3) that conversion implies.

## The Spirit and the body

Paul introduces the Holy Spirit into the equation when he says, "anyone united to the Lord becomes one spirit with him" (1 Cor. 6:17). By the work of the Spirit, the believer's spirit has been joined with Christ.[62] Thus, the body of each individual believer becomes "a temple of the Holy Spirit within you, which you have from God" (v. 19). Previously, Paul used this image of the Spirit-filled temple to highlight the sanctity of the local congregation (3:16–17). Now Paul warns about desecrating the bodies individually consecrated to God in Christ by the Spirit's presence.

The close link between spirit and body in verses 17 and 19 shows again that we belong to the Lord as a totality. Body and spirit cannot be separated. The body cannot be used in a way that is contrary to God's will without impairing the spiritual union with Christ made possible by his redemptive work (vv. 19–20). Hence the warning to "Flee from sexual immorality" (v. 18; cf. 10:14). The implication is that the believer is to take decisive action to avoid everything covered by the word *porneia*, although the immediate context is the particular example of heterosexual prostitution. The positive alternative is to "glorify God in your body" (v. 20, Gk. *doxasate;* cf. 10:31). We are to honor God by using our bodies in the way that he directs.

Some commentators have argued that the words "every sin that a person commits is outside the body" (v. 18) are Paul's own. However, it seems more likely in the flow of the argument that this is the third Corinthian slogan.[63] Paul's response is to affirm that the sexually immoral person "sins against his own body" (NIV). Thus, he grounds his prohibition of sexual immorality "in three distinct but closely related arguments (vv. 15, 16–18, 19–20) relating respectively to Christ-violation, body-violation and Spirit-violation."[64] Sexual sin is profoundly self-destructive, but not just from an individual or psychological perspective. The interlocking elements of Paul's argument show that it can destroy the person's relationship with Christ.

## Practical implications

Far from devaluing sex, Paul perceived the sexual act as "one of intimacy and *self-commitment which involved the whole person;* not the mere manipulation of some 'peripheral' function of the body."[65] Of course, people do engage in sexual activity in a manipulative and impersonal way. A rape situation would be the most destructive example of this. Paul's point is not that any kind of sexual union makes the participants "one flesh." Rather, the joining of bodies is a violation of God's purpose for sex unless it is an expression of the exclusive commitment of a man and woman in marriage, according to the pattern of Genesis 2:24. Moreover, for the Christian, sexual union outside the commitment of heterosexual marriage is a misuse of the Spirit-indwelt body that belongs to the Lord. It is an unholy act.

Gordon Fee helpfully concludes his comments on 1 Corinthians 6 with this observation:

Those who take Scripture seriously are not prudes or legalists at this point; rather, they recognize that God has purchased us for

higher things. Our bodies belong to God through the redemption of the cross; and they are destined for resurrection. Part of
the reason why Christians flee sexual immorality is that their
bodies are for the Lord, who is to be honored in the deeds of the
body as well as in other behavior and attitudes.[66]

# Overall conclusions

What, then, are the continuities between the Old and New
Testaments with regard to holiness and sexuality?

## *The nature of holiness*

In both Testaments, holiness is a *status* conferred by God on
those he has redeemed and drawn to himself. It is also a *calling* to be lived out in obedience to his word, separate from the
world and its values. Holiness is an expression of the covenant
relationship in which God has placed us. We are to bear witness to a fallen world of God's character and intentions for
humanity by our distinctive, God-determined lifestyle.

## *The parameters of holiness*

The Mosaic law, in which issues of sexual behavior and interpersonal relationships are central, establishes the parameters
of holiness for Israel. But the prescriptions of the law with
regard to sexuality actually reflect the fundamental principles of Genesis about God's purposes in creation. Jesus and
his apostles then establish the parameters of holiness under
the new covenant. They affirm again the foundational intentions of God for marriage and sexuality, as reflected in the
creation narratives and the provisions of the Mosaic law.

Although Christians are not under the law, those "who
walk not according to the flesh but according to the Spirit"

(Rom. 8:4) fulfill the law's essential requirement under the new covenant. New Testament teaching on sexuality and holiness is often given with reference to particular situations in the early church. The principles enunciated are above and beyond situational variables, however, because they are rooted in the clear and unequivocal position of the Old Testament.

The Apostle Paul was relaxed about abandoning biblical regulations concerning circumcision, sacrificial rituals, and food laws, but not concerning matters of sexual conduct. "For these were understood to be based on God's purpose for humanity in creation and not on his temporal election of Israel as a distinct group among the nations."[67] Put another way, the fulfillment of God's saving purpose for Israel and the nations in Christ demanded the relaxation of the former regulations, but not the latter.

## The penalty for unholiness

The immediate penalty for serious cases of sexual misbehavior among professing Christians is excommunication, or exclusion from the fellowship of believers until repentance has been expressed (1 Cor. 5:1–5). The ultimate penalty for persistent sexual misbehavior is divine exclusion from the kingdom of God (1 Cor. 6:9–10).

# 3

# Same-Sex Unions and Romans 1

## David Peterson

> The desire to bless same-sex unions often arises from a serious
> and sincere pastoral concern for the well-being of members of
> Christ's body. Yet those who reject the blessing of same-sex
> unions can be motivated by a pastoral concern which is equally
> serious and sincere.[68]

Although the international Lambeth Conference, held in
Canterbury, England in 1998, confirmed the traditional
Anglican/Episcopalian view that all homosexual practice is
"incompatible with Scripture," there continue to be serious
debates in the Anglican communion about this position.
Jeffrey John's 1993 publication *"Permanent, Faithful, Stable"
Christian Same-Sex Partnerships* was reissued in 2000, and
Rowan Williams' 1989 lecture for the Lesbian and Gay
Christian Movement, entitled *The Body's Grace,* was repub-
lished in booklet form in 2002, immediately following his
appointment as Archbishop of Canterbury. Since Lambeth,
there has been a furor over the decision of the Canadian dio-
cese of New Westminster to allow the blessing of same-sex
unions and in America over the election of a practicing
homosexual as bishop of New Hampshire. In England, the

proposal that Jeffrey John should be made bishop of Reading was greeted with such opposition that, courageously, he asked for his appointment not to proceed.

Similar debates are taking place in other Christian denominations throughout the world. This chapter will focus specifically on the Anglican context as a case study of this widespread controversy. I am grateful to the Most Reverend Drexel Wellington Gomez, Archbishop of the West Indies, for commissioning the writing of the booklet, *True Union in the Body? A Contribution to the Discussion within the Anglican Communion Concerning the Public Blessing of Same-Sex Unions.* The authors deal most helpfully with the biblical, ethical, pastoral, and political issues – and in a remarkably concise way. In what follows I will critique more fully the approach of Jeffrey John and Rowan Williams with reference to the interpretation of Romans 1.

# A novel approach

## A desire-based approach to sexuality

Rowan Williams highlights the virtues of celibacy but opposes the notion that homosexual orientation necessitates the celibate life. Without considering the scriptural challenge to abstinence on the part of *all* who are single, he advocates a desire-based approach to sexuality. Where there is genuine desire for another person, there is authentic sexual activity, regardless of orientation.[69] He argues that in the Bible there is "a good deal to steer us away from assuming that reproductive sex is a norm, however important and theologically significant it may be."[70] He further suggests that,

the absolute condemnation of same-sex relations of intimacy must rely either on an abstract fundamentalist deployment of a number of very ambiguous texts, or on a problematic and non-scriptural theory about natural complementarity, applied narrowly and crudely to physical differentiation without regard to psychological structures.[71]

The preceding chapters have argued that the traditional Christian position is not simply based on a few "very ambiguous texts." There is consistent biblical teaching about sexuality and holiness and God's purpose for human beings in creation. What is said about homosexuality in Scripture must be read within this theological framework. Robert Gagnon, in his recent and thorough reexamination of the evidence, has shown that the texts are not as ambiguous as Rowan Williams suggests.[72] The contributors to *True Union in the Body?* conclude that, "Those texts carry the weight they do because they represent the *uniform* testimony of Scripture and are part of a wider theologically formed understanding of homosexuality."[73]

We devote an entire chapter to the consideration of Romans 1:18–27 because of the attention this text receives in the arguments mounted by Jeffrey John and other advocates of same-sex partnerships. While there has been legitimate debate about the homosexual activity mentioned in 1 Corinthians 6:9,[74] advocates of the traditional Catholic and Protestant position have consistently argued that their position is well grounded in the argument of Romans 1:18–27. A new approach, however, has now challenged that position.

## A theological model for gay relationships

Jeffrey John argues on two fronts. His first aim is to convince the mainstream church that "a faithful homosexual relationship is not 'incompatible with scripture' (certainly no more so than the remarriage of the divorced, or the leadership of women, which are far more 'incompatible' with the Bible's plainest meaning)."[75] He does not intend to jettison the traditional, biblical theology of sex and marriage, but rather to extend it to include gay people. His second aim is to persuade gay people that "contrary to the usual assumptions, the gospel has something positive to say about gay relationships, and that those who live in them belong to the Church as much as anyone else."[76]

We must certainly affirm that the gospel has something positive to say to gay people. Christians need to beware of homophobia in all its sinful forms and manifestations. In positive terms, we must be welcoming towards those who struggle with their sexuality. But what Jeffrey John offers is actually a denial of the grace and power of the gospel for homosexuals. It is also a distortion of biblical teaching about sexuality and holiness and a misreading of the relationship between Christ and the church.

John's fundamental argument is that, in biblical terms, human sexuality is not exclusively or necessarily intended for procreation; "it is also intended to express a covenant commitment between two people which is holy because it reflects God's covenanted love for us, and gives us a framework for learning to love in his image."[77] Rowan Williams takes a similar position in *The Body's Grace.*

There is an element of truth in this idea, but the development of the argument takes us so far away from the Bible's teaching that it stands in contradiction to what God has revealed. The element of truth is that human sexuality is not simply intended for procreation. The one-flesh union of a man and a woman in Genesis 2:18–24 is clearly ordained "for the mutual society, help, and comfort, that the one ought to have of the other, both in prosperity and adversity."[78] But this union cannot be divorced from the commission to humanity as male and female in Genesis 1:27–28 to "be fruitful and multiply and fill the earth." Genesis 2 cannot be disconnected from Genesis 1. Of course marriages flourish without procreation.

Throughout Scripture, however, the joy and fulfillment of sexual union continues to be limited to permanent and faithful male and female partnerships.

Marriage is a model of the relationship between Christ and the church, a metaphor developed most clearly in Ephesians 5:25–33. However, sexual union is not at the heart of this comparison. The love of Christ in his self-sacrificing care for the church is the model for husbands, and the submission of the church to that loving headship is the model for wives.

Any genuine Christian relationship will express the sort of commitment between two people which is a reflection of God's love for us. All Christians ought to pursue permanent, faithful, and stable relationships, in friendships as well as in marriage. However, holiness is compromised if relationships involve sexual intimacy outside the commitment of heterosexual marriage. So we cannot argue that unmarried people lack anything in their relationship with God if they are deprived of sexual intimacy with another human being. The biblical argument works the other way around. Those who are married are called to conform every aspect of their union, including the sexual, to the model of Christ and his church.

## Misusing Scripture

Jeffrey John accuses evangelicals of misusing Scripture, and his challenge needs to be taken seriously. The current debate calls for a reevaluation of the interpretative process used with respect to other matters, such as divorce and remarriage and the ordination of women. John's easy dismissal of the references to homosexual behavior in Leviticus, however, is based on a supposed late dating of the passages and highly speculative arguments about "the author's special concern to encourage childbirth" and "to counter syncretism."[79] He also trivializes the hermeneutical question about the moral force of the Levitical rules for Christians and does not consider issues regarding holiness and wholeness that are highlighted in Chapters 1 and 2, above.

With respect to the Pauline material, John argues that 1 Corinthians 6:9 and 1 Timothy 1:10 mention homosexuality in passing, "within conventional sin-lists, probably taken over from Hellenistic Jewish sources."[80] He concludes that prostitution and pederasty are the forms of homosexuality that were likely to be uppermost in Paul's mind, not the kind of faithful and stable relationships being argued by Jeffrey John. However, the presumption that Paul could not have considered the possibility of permanent same-sex relationships needs to be challenged.

## Evidence from the Greco-Roman world

The understanding that homosexual behavior arises from a disposition – the result of nature or nurture – did not simply arise in the nineteenth century with the development of modern psychiatry. "Homosexuality" was a disposition known in the world of the first century AD, and there are words in many ancient languages to describe people who engage recurrently in same-sex activity. However, in Chapter 5 of this book, David Field (following Joel Garver) warns against assuming that "homosexuality" or "being gay," on the psychological, emotional, and experiential level, is some kind of unified phenomenon either within our own time and culture or over time and among cultures.

Bruce Thornton's research points to evidence from Aristotle, Plato, and Aristophanes for "the ancient Greek belief that homosexuals are born and not made."[81] David Greenberg argues that "Physiological explanations for homosexual desire or distinct homosexual roles have a long pedigree, dating back to the world of classical antiquity. Psychological explanations are not exactly new either."[82]

Bernadette Brooten's analysis of lesbianism in the ancient world leads her to conclude that Paul may well have known of homosexual orientation. She opposes the view that Paul condemns only heterosexuals committing homosexual acts and not homosexuals *per se*, and she shows how the distinction between sexual orientation and sexual acts could have made sense to him. She found that "some ancient writers saw particular same-sex acts as symptoms of a chronic disease that affected the entirety of one's identity."[83] Her study of ancient astrological texts shows that astrologers recognized a variety of preferences, which they linked to the stars. So she concludes that,

> Paul could have believed that *tribades, kinaidoi,* and other sexually unorthodox persons were born that way and yet still condemn them as unnatural and shameful, this all the more so since he is speaking of groups of people rather than of individuals.[84]

## The significance for the debate of Romans 1:18–27

Jeffrey John argues that Romans 1:18–27 is the most important text to be considered, because it is "the only place where we have anything like a theological argument against homosexual practice."[85] He rightly observes that Paul is engaging here in an attack on Gentile idolatry. However, it should also be noted that many commentators see a deliberate echo of the Adam narratives in Genesis 2–3, with an implied indictment of the whole of humanity. Israel is specifically included in this because the language in verse 23 reflects Psalm 106 (LXX 105):20, referring to the idolatry of Israel (cf. Jer. 2:11; Isa. 44:9–20).[86] Jeffrey John goes on to observe that, because of this perverse rejection of God, God has abandoned them to dishonorable passions exemplified in the exchange of heterosexual intercourse for homosexual, and to a base mind and improper conduct exemplified in a long list of sins deserving death. It is the particular way in which John understands "the exchange of heterosexual intercourse for homosexual" that we must now address.

# Idolatry, impurity, and the wrath of God (Rom. 1:18–27)

The error identified in Romans 1:18–27 is the human pattern of suppressing the truth about God and worshipping a god of our own devising. God expresses his wrath by abandoning humanity to the consequences of this rebellion. Paul draws attention to the immediate implication of this in terms of the misuse of sex and every form of anti-social and destructive behavior (vv. 28–32). In that context, homosexual activity is singled out, but not as an analysis of individual experience or to provide the psychological profile of those who engage in same-sex intercourse. His concern is societal and general – a portrait of fallen humanity. Homoeroticism is a symptom of the original rebellion of humanity against God. It does not affirm God's creation purpose for male and female as the image of God but is a sign of the disruption of the order of creation brought about by the fall of humanity, as portrayed in Genesis 3.

## *Idolatry and sexual promiscuity*

Paul's purpose in Romans 1:18 – 3:20 is to show that "so absolute is sin's power over people that only God's power, available in the gospel, can rescue them."[87] This section of the letter sits between a brief statement of the gospel's purpose in 1:16–17 and the fuller exposition of its content and achievement in 3:21–31. The gospel is necessary because "the wrath of God is revealed from heaven against all ungodliness and wickedness of those who by their wickedness suppress the truth" (1:18). The truth in question is "what can be known about God" through his self-revelation in the created order (1:19–20). Even apart from the special revelation found in Scripture, human beings are therefore "without excuse." "For though they knew God, they did not honor him as God or give thanks to him, but they became futile in their thinking, and their senseless minds were darkened" (1:21). Sin is a failure to give God the glory that is due to him and to acknowledge that all the good things we enjoy come from his hand.[88]

Sin expresses itself essentially in what is three times described as an "exchange" (using some form of the Greek verb *allassō*). People exchange "the glory of the immortal God for images resembling a mortal human being or birds or four-footed animals or reptiles" (1:23).[89] This is further explained in terms of exchanging the truth about God for (lit.) "the lie" of idolatry and worshipping and serving "the creature rather than the Creator" (1:25). Distortion of the truth about God then leads to a distortion of the truth about humanity made in the image and likeness of God. The other exchange, which we shall now consider in some detail, is that of "natural intercourse for unnatural" (1:26–7).

It should not be concluded from this argument that Paul is only considering homosexual behavior which is the direct result of engagement with idolatrous worship. The more general picture of verse 24 could apply to any kind of sexual impurity, and the catalogue of vices in verses 28–31 goes way beyond any cultic setting. In each of the three paragraphs beginning with the expression "God gave them up" (vv. 24–25, 26–27, and 28–32), Paul is portraying the situation of humanity in rebellion against God. Individuals will pursue different patterns of disobedience, and not all will be directly connected with explicit idolatry. Homosexual acts and the various behaviors listed at the end of the chapter are particular indications of the general truth outlined in verses 19–23, namely that we are a race in rebellion against our Creator.

## Sexual promiscuity and the wrath of God

When Paul writes that "God gave them up" (vv. 24, 26, 28), he is expressing in another way the fact that "the wrath of God is revealed from heaven against all ungodliness and wickedness of those who by their wickedness suppress the truth" (v. 18). Beginning with Adam, human beings have characteristically turned their backs on a relationship with God in order to pursue their own agenda. God's response has been to "hand over" (Gk. *paredōken*) the race to a form of judgement that is appropriate to this rejection. The present expression of the wrath of God is only an anticipation of the judgement to come (2:3–5, 8–9, 16).[90]

Paul first speaks of people being handed over "in the lusts of their hearts to impurity, to the dishonouring of their bodies among themselves" (1:24). This cannot be taken to mean that God actually impelled people to sin. The expression "in the lusts of their hearts" describes the condition they were *in* as a result of turning away from God (1:21–3). The state *into which* they are delivered is impurity (Gk. *eis akatharsian*). The result or the implication of this is "the dishonouring of their bodies among themselves" (Gk. *tou atimazesthai*). Here the apostle speaks quite generally about the abuse of God's glory leading to the abuse of other people in a sexual way. "Human respect (both self-respect and respect for others) is rooted in the recognition that only God has authority as Creator to order and dispose of that which is created."[91]

In the next reference, however, the focus narrows to homosexual behavior. God gave them up "to dishonourable passions," as then specifically described: "For their women exchanged natural relations for those that are contrary to nature; and the men likewise gave up natural relations with women and were consumed with passion for one another, men committing shameless acts with men and receiving in themselves the due penalty for their error" (1:26–7).

### The homosexual "exchange"

Echoes of Genesis 1 in these verses highlight the distortion of the Creator's intention for humanity that same-sex intercourse involves. Instead of the nouns "man" and "woman," adjectives found in Genesis 1:27 LXX, meaning "male" and "female" (Gk. *arsenes* and *thēleiai*), are used to highlight the sexual differentiation involved in God's creation of humanity (cf. Matt. 19:4; Mark 10:6; Gal. 3:28). In this context, "natural relations" (Gk. *tēn physikēn chrēsin*, lit. "the natural use") and "those that are contrary to nature" (Gk. *tēn para physin*, lit. "the unnatural [use]") will refer to sexual behavior that is "in accordance with the intention of the Creator" and "contrary to the intention of the Creator," respectively.[92]

Reviewing the way extrabiblical Jewish writers of the period considered same-sex intercourse, Robert Gagnon argues that "minimally, Paul is referring to the anatomical and procreative complementarity of male and female."[93] For Paul it was a simple matter of observation that homosexual intercourse was "contrary to nature," so that pagans who were ignorant of the biblical record had no excuse for not knowing God's purpose for the sexual organs.

Some modern writers have argued that Romans 1:26–27 refers to what is "natural" for the individuals concerned. They note that Paul elsewhere uses the word "nature" to describe things the way they are by reason of their intrinsic state or birth (e.g., Rom. 2:14; 11:21, 24; Gal. 2:15; 4:8; Eph. 2:3).[94] Thus, Michael Vasey proposed that Paul condemns those who are "naturally" heterosexual if they engage in homosexual acts but not those who are "naturally" homosexual.[95] Jeffrey John argues that "against nature" means "against the order of nature itself," but also "that it is against the person's *own* nature."⁹⁶ This argument seems confusing, since the issue of "the order of nature itself" (alluding to the Creator's plan) seems to override the issue of one's own nature (expressing human fallenness).

John argues that "Paul does not recognize a separate category of homosexual people but only homosexual acts." He goes on to conclude that Paul "takes it for granted that homosexual behavior is a free, perverse choice on the part of 'naturally' heterosexual men and women." However, the text does not necessarily assume that those in question were actually having heterosexual relations and then gave them up for homosexual relations. Such people are doubtless included in Paul's perspective, but his reference is more comprehensive and general than that.

Furthermore, Paul is not simply describing a pattern of individual choice, but rather demonstrating that the consequences of humanity's rebellion and God's wrath against "all ungodliness and wickedness" have a societal and whole-culture impact. Of course there is individual culpability for each of the sins mentioned in the passage, but Paul's main point is to indicate how God's wrath can be discerned and why our fallenness leaves us all in such a desperate situation.

One particular example of this is God's abandonment of certain people to the consequences of their perverted choice in the sexual realm. Literally translated, Romans 1:27 speaks of males who "abandoned the natural use of the female and were inflamed in their desire for one another." The reference is not to what is natural for such people in terms of their particular sexual orientation, but literally what is "the natural use of the female" for the male in the created order. By implication, "the natural use (of the male)" by the female is meant in 1:26. The word *chrēsis* ("use") for sexual intercourse is well established in Greek literature of the time.⁹⁷

Although Paul is concerned with homosexual *acts*, regardless of "orientation," it must be remembered that the clause in Romans 1:26 is a description of "sinful passions" (Gk. *pathē atimias,* lit. "dishonourable passions," ESV). This phrase parallels "the lusts of their hearts" (v. 24) and indicates that homosexual *desires* must be included with every other desire that is contrary to God's will.[98] Paul is concerned with improper and misdirected passions, whatever the cause. These lead to the sort of behavior he condemns.

Only Romans 1 in the New Testament identifies and condemns female homosexual behavior along with male homosexual behavior. This provides strong evidence that "Paul was not simply critiquing homosexual acts which were oppressive, pederastic or cultic. His critique operates at a more fundamental level."[99] The reference in both cases is quite general and without qualification. The focus is on behavior, not orientation. Having exchanged natural relations for unnatural relations, they are "consumed with passion for one another" and commit "shameless acts" (Gk. *tēn aschēmosynēn,* lit. "the shameless [deed]").[100] Thus, they receive in themselves "the due penalty for their error." This last expression probably refers to "their sexual perversion itself as the punishment for their abandonment of the true God,"[101] rather than implying some unspecified punishment for their sexual behavior.

## Conclusions from Romans 1

1. Romans 1 stresses the self-degrading and shameful character of both idolatry and same-sex intercourse. Paul gives other examples of the serious consequences of humanity's rebellion against God (vv. 28–31), but he particularly mentions idolatry and homosexual activity because they represent that *exchange* of the truth about God and his purposes for a lie that is at the heart of sin.

2. Paul does not explain the genesis of homosexuality in the experience of *individuals* in terms of idolatry leading to

same-sex intercourse. Rather, "he is speaking in terms of collective entities, not individuals, and in terms of widespread effect, not origin."[102] Intertextual echoes of Genesis 1 – 2 in Romans 1 indicate that "both idolatry and same-sex intercourse reject God's verdict that what was made and arranged was 'very good' (Gen. 1:31)."[103]

3. It is a misuse of the canon of Scripture to say that Romans 1 allows for same-sex unions, when the rest of the Bible is consistently clear about God's will with respect to sexual intercourse. Anglicans in particular are bound by Article 20 of the Articles of Religion in the *Book of Common Prayer* (1662) not to "ordain any thing that is contrary to God's Word written," nor to "so expound one place of Scripture, that it be repugnant to another."

4. To suggest that "natural use" in Romans 1:26 could include the sort of behavior condemned elsewhere in Scripture as being contrary to God's will would be to disregard the principle of contextual analysis. The passage highlights humanity's failure to respond appropriately to the revelation of God's character and will in the created order. One aspect of our fallenness – namely a homosexual orientation – cannot be used to justify disobedience to God's will as it is revealed in both the natural order and in Scripture.

## The hope of the gospel

Romans 8:18–25 makes it clear that humanity's rebellion against God has affected the natural order, which awaits its ultimate transformation when God's people will experience the redemption of their bodies. Meanwhile, Romans 3 speaks about justification by faith and redemption through Christ's atoning work. Romans 4 – 8 tell us how to live faithfully and expectantly before God, in the light of Christ's death and resurrection and in anticipation of the final outworking of

God's purpose in the new creation. Paul affirms that we were saved in this hope (8:24). Romans 1 must not, therefore, be read in isolation, but rather in the light of the hope that the rest of Romans unfolds.

# 4

# Radical Disorientation

## Fallen Sexuality and the Christian Doctrine of Sin (I)

### David Field

Many of the advocates of unqualified acceptance of homosexuality seem to be operating with a simplistic anthropology that assumes that whatever is must be good: they have a theology of creation but no theology of sin and redemption.[104]

## Introduction

It is the argument of this chapter that the wickedness, folly, and tragedy of sin are to be measured by the holiness, wisdom, and overflowing goodness of God. Sin is theologically defined as an assault upon God and upon his authority and purpose. This means that sin is both deicidal and, since humankind is made in the image of God, suicidal. God is life, love, and truth, and thus sin as the rejection of life is the embrace of death, as the rejection of love is the embrace of loathing, and as the rejection of truth is the embrace of falsehood. Examining fallen sexuality and, in particular, homosexual fallenness, in the light of these theological truths about sin serves both to clarify and confirm our understanding of sin. This exercise also provides fresh perspectives upon the radical disorientation that is, and that leads to, fallen sexuality.

## Assumptions

The key assumption upon which this exploration proceeds is that the Bible teaches that all homosexual sexual acts are sinful. Determined efforts have been made, particularly over the last thirty years or so, to demonstrate that this assumption is unwarranted. Yet all readings of the scriptural data which suggest that the Bible does not condemn all homosexual sexual acts have a strong air of special pleading about them. Robert Gagnon's recent work, *The Bible and Homosexual Practice,* is a particularly compelling corrective to this sort of hermeneutical gymnastics.[105] Gagnon summarizes,

> First, there is clear, strong, and credible evidence that the Bible unequivocally defines same-sex intercourse as sin. Second, there exist no valid hermeneutical arguments, derived from either general principles of biblical interpretation or contemporary scientific knowledge and experience, for overriding the Bible's authority on this matter. In sum, the Bible presents the anatomical, sexual, and procreative complementarity of male and female as clear and convincing proof of God's will for sexual unions. . . . Thus same-sex intercourse constitutes an inexcusable rebellion against the intentional design of the created order.[106]

And again,

> Same-sex intercourse is strongly and unequivocally rejected by the revelation of Scripture.[107]

Richard B. Hays concludes that "the NT remains unambiguous and univocal in its condemnation of homosexual conduct."[108] And Wolfhart Pannenberg judges that

> If a church were to let itself be pushed to the point where it ceased to treat homosexual activity as a departure from the biblical norm, and recognized homosexual unions as a personal partnership of love equivalent to marriage, such a church would no longer stand on biblical ground but against the unequivocal witness of Scripture. A church that took this step would cease to be the one, holy, catholic, and apostolic church.[109]

Other assumptions underlying this chapter are more briefly stated. First, all who write on issues relating to homosexuality should recognize that their judgement of these matters is liable to distortion by reason of their "own different but often more severe disabilities."[110] Our attempts to face up to the irrationalities and hypocrisies inside us all will never be wholly successful. Second, discussions of homosexuality are, in Jeffrey Satinover's words, "personally harrowing, scientifically complicated, and politically controversial."[111] The literature upon the subject is complex and vast, and it is almost impossible to state matters with the degree of theological precision, intellectual clarity, and personal sensitivity necessary to avoid giving unintended offense. The Ramsay Colloquium[112] was preemptively robust:

> We are well aware that this declaration will be dismissed by some as a display of "homophobia," but such dismissals have become unpersuasive and have ceased to intimidate. Indeed, we do not think it a bad thing that people should experience a reflexive recoil from what is wrong. To achieve such a recoil is precisely the point of moral education of the young. What we have tried to do here is to bring this reflexive and often pre-articulate recoil to reasonable expression.[113]

Yet what constitutes "reasonable expression" on the one hand, and "pre-articulate recoil" on the other, is a matter of widely varying judgement and thus, regrettably, it is an assumption that some readers will find elements of what follows disturbing in ways which the author sincerely does not intend. In particular, imprecise articulation of Scripture's condemnation of sin may come across as expressing personal animus rather than wise and gracious divine disapproval.

A final assumption is methodological. It is that of the propriety of the argument *ex convenientia* in theological matters. This works by providing a description, from a variety of angles, of key elements of the author's conclusion or conclusions (in this case, among others, that homosexual acts are sinful). As this description is given, the suggestive force, explanatory power, and sheer "fittingness" of the conclusion themselves constitute an argument without the author actually proceeding step by step through the statement and arrangement of a number of premises and conclusions. Thus, this chapter and the next will attempt what Robert Jenson calls "some display of the fact of sin in a few of its aspects."[114] The hope is that a survey and reminder of some of the fundamental biblical perspectives upon sin will add clarity, perspective, and precision to our understanding of the specific phenomena of fallen sexuality, and in particular, of homosexual sin.[115]

# Sin is theologically defined

## *Ethical norms*

All ethical judgements presuppose norms, criteria, and standards by which behaviors can be measured. "Where there is no law, neither is there violation" (Rom. 4:15). Whether we call the homophobe evil, the pedophile sick, the zoosexual abnormal, or the adulterer unfaithful, we are applying ethical norms.[116] The source and authority of those norms are, of course, foundational issues in ethics. And for the Christian, there can be no doubt about either. God, the holy and loving sovereign Creator, is the source and authority of ethical norms.

"What is sin?" the catechumen is asked. And the reply is plain: "Sin is any want of conformity unto, or transgression of, the law of God."[117] The psalmist declares, "Against you, you alone, have I sinned, and done what is evil in your sight" (Ps. 51:4). And the apostles tell us the same: "All have sinned and fall short of the glory of God" and "sin is lawlessness" (Rom. 3:23; 1 John 3:4).

Moreover, God does not arbitrarily impose these laws or norms, the transgression of which constitute sin. Rather, the laws flow from and perfectly express his righteous and good character and his wise and gracious purpose. Thus sin is not only the rejection of God's authority as Creator and lawgiver; it is also a rejection of that character and purpose. God's authority lies behind his rule; his character and his purpose reveal the good. And humankind in sin seeks alternate rule and alternate good – another lord and another savior.

The first chapter of Romans, which as we have seen is a key passage in consideration of homosexuality, makes this rejection altogether clear. Human sins flow from human sinfulness and human sinfulness, at root, is a religious issue. Sin is, first of all, the suppression of the truth of God, the refusal to worship God, the failure to give thanks to God. Worshipping the creature, engaging in homosexual activity, and all other sinful acts flow from and express the turning from God which is the heart of sin.

## Sin gets messy

The fundamental biblical perspective upon sin, then, is that it is to be theologically defined.[118] And we may add that the sheer depth and complexity of sin in the human person derive from the fact that humans have been made in the image of God. As obedient son, Adam was a mirror in which the radiance of God's glory and the imprint of God's character were to be seen. A mirror regarded merely as a physical object may have just a few millimeters' depth yet, regarded as the bearer of an image, it will have the depth of that which it reflects. The mirror will have the depth of a yard when a yard-rule is set against it and the depth of a mile when placed at the beginning of a mile-long path. Since Adam was created for God's glory – that is, to reflect and represent the perfections of an infinite God – then Adam, though finite as a creature, was to have infinite depth in relation to God as mirror. Thus the damage and distress and disorder of sin will also have incomprehensible "depth" in the sinner. In sin, things can go wrong and get complicated in an infinite number of ways, and the rejection of the infinite God causes almost infinite chaos and tragedy in the human person.

# Sin is deicidal

## *Idolatry*

It is for this reason that idolatry is at the heart of the sin-project. The rejection of God's authoritative norms, holy character, and loving purpose is not done in a vacuum: it implies a preference for alternate authority, character, and purpose. This alternate authority, character, and purpose derive from, or perhaps even constitute, a rival god, the idol. The sinner's turn from his Maker is inevitably and invariably a turn to a false god – whether identified as and with Satan, self, the world disconnected from its Creator, the powers, the works of our hands, or something else.

## Deicide

Thus the replacement of the true God with gods of the sinner's own design, construction, and appointment, is at the heart of sin. "Idolatry is not an accident, as if some of us just happened to hit on wrong candidates for deity."[119] As the Puritans, and not just the Puritans, would have it, sin is *deicidal*. The sinner refuses to love God's holy character, to believe God's authoritative revelation, to trust God's loving intentions, and to obey God's righteous commands.[120] And the refusal to love is expressed biblically as a hatred of God. "All who do evil hate the light" (John 3:20). "No one can serve two masters; for a slave will either hate the one and love the other, or be devoted to the one and despise the other. You cannot serve God and wealth" (Matt. 6:24). "The mind that is set on the flesh is hostile to God" (Rom. 8:7).

## Forms of the hatred of God

This hatred of God and the desire to do away with him take various forms.[121] Against God's triune being, sin wishes to assert the ultimacy of the one *or* the ultimacy of the many. Against God's law, sin sets up rival standards and norms. Rivaling God's authority, sin is simultaneously anarchic and tyrannical. As revolutionary idolatry, it distorts the gifts of God and then celebrates the distortion as the means to renewal and freedom, an alternative salvation. Suppressing God's truth, sin exchanges this truth for a lie and causes us to become confused and uncertain about humanness and the world around as well as about God himself.[122] Rejecting God's purpose and, therefore, his ordering of means to ends, sin seeks alternative uses for what God has made.

> Component parts of the sexual revolution . . . have in common the
> presuppositions that the body is little more than an instrument

for the fulfillment of desire, and that the fulfillment of desire is the essence of the self.[123]

All sins give evidence of this distortion and, therefore, homo-sexual sins do too. As Hays puts it, Paul

> adduces the fact of widespread homosexual behavior as evi-dence that human beings are indeed in rebellion against their Creator [. . . and homosexual intercourse is . . .] a particularly graphic image of the way in which human fallenness distorts God's created order.[124]

So it is, then, that an essential element of the self-awareness of the sinner is the recognition that, so far as a human being is a sinner, that far he is a hater of God. That the unbeliever refuses to believe this, and that the humble are humbled by it, are ironies of the truth with profound consequences for Christian evangelism and spirituality.

# Sin is suicidal

## *The image of God*

At this point, however, the picture is far from complete. Humankind has been created in the image of God.[125] Developed throughout the Bible, the concept certainly con-tains the idea that humankind has been created in order to represent and reflect the glory of God both consciously and obediently. The Apostle Paul, for example, closely connects the ideas of image and glory. God's creation of all things is an outflow of his infinitely good character and a display of his perfections and this, in part, is what is meant by the assertion that God has made all things for his glory. But whereas lions and lettuce, and mountains and comets, and oceans and insects and stars display the perfections of God unconsciously, the calling of humankind is to represent and reflect God's good and holy character in conscious obedience to his righteous command. Obedience means glory-bearing; disobedience means shame. Sin *is* the "inglorious exchange."[126]

## Loving and hating God; loving and hating self

For Adam, to love God's character, recognize his authority, and embrace his purpose would have meant that he rejected sin. He would need and desire no other standard and calling than God's loving holiness, expressed in his good and righteous commands and promises. He would not want to do away with or replace God. Rather, he would love God with his whole being. Vitally, this in turn means that Adam would love himself.

But, as we have seen, Adam, as sinner, hated God. Ironically, made as he was in the image of God, Adam was already "like God." But not content with bearing God's glory, reflecting and representing God's character, recognizing God's authority, embracing God's purpose, and obeying God's commands, Adam grasped at equality with God. This was his fall, his shame. Determined to do away with God and the reflection of God that he saw in his own being and calling, he took a hammer to himself as mirror and shattered the image of God. When, in sin, he looked at himself and saw the image of God, shattered yet not obliterated, he hated himself as he hated God. Because he was designed perfectly in the image of God, so far as Adam loved God he would love himself as the mirror of God. When he embraced sin, the situation was reversed. Looking at himself as a sinner, Adam hated the vestiges of the image of God and thus hated himself. And all in Adam die the same death of brokenness and self-loathing.

## Consistency in sin would be murder, madness, and suicide

The unregenerate who was true to himself (that is to say, fully consistent as a God-hater), would sin without limit. But unlimited sin would be simultaneous madness, murder, and suicide.[127] Madness, because reality is filled with God and the consistent sinner flees from reality: God is truth and the consistent sinner, endeavoring to do away with God, would reject truth. Yet truth is one, though lies are many, and so the rejection of truth, consistently worked through, would be a complete disconnection with reality. Murder, because all other human persons are image-bearers and the consistent sinner, seeking to murder God and yet unable to do so, would, instead and as well, do all in his power to cleanse the planet of every sign of God (Titus 3:3). Every other human person must be killed. Suicide, because the fully consistent sinner would, regarding the remaining image of God upon himself and hating that image, seek to destroy himself. Hating God, the sinner hates truth, love, and life, embraces falsehood, hatred, and death and so, unrestrained, would plunge into madness, murder, and suicide.

## God keeps us from consistency

God's mercy is such, however, that he restrains the sin of those who hate him, holding them back from full consistency. Thus we can see that all around us, though only in part, the unregenerate accept truth, obey commands, reject evil, love others, and cherish life. The Christian doctrine of "total depravity" teaches that sin has corrupted every dimension and faculty of human life: it does not teach that every sinner is as evil as he or she could possibly be.

And thus the sinner is divided, a self-alienated person. Put simply, the two "selves" of the fallen human person are first the sinner as sinner, the God-hating self; and second the sinner as restrained, the residual image-bearer. This division sets up four relationships and stances within the one human person (see Fig. 4.1).

Adam (representing all sinners) the God-hater perceives himself as a God-hater and loves this self.

Adam the God-hater perceives himself as Adam the residual image-bearer and hates this self.

Adam the residual image-bearer perceives himself as Adam the God-hater and hates this self.

Adam the residual image-bearer perceives himself as Adam the image-bearer and loves this self.

Only unfallen Adam, Jesus of Nazareth, and the fully restored people of God know the undivided self. All other human experience is that of self-alienation and of consequent confusion, fear, anger, and guilt.

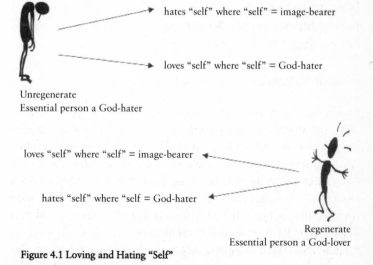

hates "self" where "self" = image-bearer

loves "self" where "self" = God-hater

Unregenerate
Essential person a God-hater

loves "self" where "self" = image-bearer

hates "self" where "self = God-hater

Regenerate
Essential person a God-lover

**Figure 4.1 Loving and Hating "Self"**

This breakdown helps to explain some of the complexities of the biblical data. Are we to love ourselves as Luke 10:27 might suggest, or to hate ourselves as Luke 14:26 indicates? Clearly, it depends upon which "self" it is that we are referring to.

## Self-love and self-hatred

Scripture teaches that one of the two "selves" is the essential, or the "true," self. Familiar alternatives express this dichotomy: in Adam or in Christ; children of darkness or children of light; under wrath or under grace; spiritually dead or spiritually raised. The renewal of the human person by the Spirit's life-giving work of uniting him to Jesus Christ changes that person from being essentially a hater-of-God to being essentially a lover-of-God. What takes place at regeneration is a fundamental change of nature. Transferred from death to life, from Adam to Christ, the human person's essential nature is transformed from that of the essential God-hater (who still bears the image of God) to the essential God-lover (who still carries around "indwelling sin").

## Continuing tension

It is important to recognize the continuing tension. It is a tension that derives from the fact that no human being, aside from Jesus of Nazareth, is wholly consistent with who he or she really is. As we have seen, God in his grace does not allow the unregenerate to be fully consistent with their essential identity as God-haters. In his wisdom, God does not purpose that the regenerate should achieve full and immediate consistency with their essential identity as God-lovers. All human beings, regenerate and unregenerate alike, live in and with the tension of not being "true to themselves." The God-hater is not fully consistent because he bears the image of God still. But he hates that image. The God-lover is not fully consistent because sin dwells in him still. But he hates that sin. Only in the new heavens and the new earth is the tension resolved.[128] The continuing tension, however, constitutes a part of the self-commending power of the axiom: the sinner, as sinner, is suicidal.

# Sin is the contradiction of life and the embrace of death

## Sinful antitheses

Thus far we have seen that to consider sin as essentially God-hating, God-defying, and God-rejecting leads to several broad conclusions about the nature of sin and the status and experience of sinners. However, a number of more specific observations arising from an understanding of the essence of sin can also be made, and it is to these that we now turn. God is in himself life and love and truth, and thus so far as sin is understood to be God-hating, God-defying, and God-rejecting, it will comprise the embrace of death, hatred, and falsehood.[129] An examination of the radical disorientation of the sinner in the fallenness of his sexuality will serve only to confirm this.

Sin is a rejection of God and is therefore the contradiction of life and the embrace of death. A number of Scripture passages make this clear:

In the day that you eat of it you shall die. (Gen. 2:17)

If you obey the commandments of the LORD your God . . . then you shall live . . . loving the LORD your God, obeying him, and

holding fast to him; for that means life to you and length of
days. (Deut. 30:16, 20)

All who hate me love death. (Prov. 8:36)

Repent and turn from all your transgressions . . . Why will you
die, O house of Israel . . . turn, then, and live. (Ezek. 18:30–32)

To set the mind on the flesh is death. (Rom. 8:6)

You were dead through the trespasses and sins in which you once
lived. (Eph. 2:1–2)

This embrace of death characterizes all sin and sins. It is
appropriate that Foucault ends the first volume of *The
History of Sexuality* with a section entitled "The Right of
Death and Power over Life," asserting that

For a long time, one of the characteristic privileges of sovereign
power was the right to decide life and death . . . [which made]
suicide . . . a way to usurp the power of death which the sovereign alone . . . had the right to exercise.[130]

## The embrace of barrenness

All sexual sin and sins confirm and illustrate sin as the embrace
of death. The sin of same-sex sexual activity is one particular
confirmation of this. That homosexual sexual activity is the
embrace of barrenness is biologically obvious but, as we shall
see, far from arising from a simplistic misapplication of natural
law theory, this observation is theologically grounded. The life
of God is a life of creative, fruitful, productive love which desires
and secures the welfare of the other and which both sustains
and satisfies those who share it. The life of sin is not, and this is
sadly all too clearly illustrated by same-sex sexual activity.

## Consequentialist arguments from the harm of homosexual activity

Two different paths could be taken from this point. One path goes on to describe the damage inflicted by homosexual lifestyles. There are truly appalling statistics relating to average life expectancy, widespread levels of physical, psychological, and emotional ill-health, the common practice of associated destructive behaviors, and the prevalence of relational instability in what is sometimes termed "the gay community."[131] These statistics are far from irrelevant: they bring home with devastating and tragic force the simple fact that sin messes up lives. Sin hurts and sin does not work.

There are dangers, however, with following this path and focusing on its effects. Rhetorically, this approach fails to recognize that "average," "widespread," "common," and "prevalence" are not universal terms, and that probabilities mean little to driven individuals. Theologically, the chief danger is that the sinfulness of sin begins to be located in the hurt it inflicts rather than in the defiance of God's holy authority and the rejection of his loving purpose which it expresses. And this consequentialist mode of argument can cut another way. If a single counterexample can be found – an example of a long, healthy, stable, loving, caring, and fulfilled life in sin – and if evil is defined as "that which hurts" and hurt is identified with immediately observable phenomena, then suddenly and clearly same-sex sexual activity is not in and of itself evil. That said, it is not only those who regard same-sex sexual activity as sinful who rely upon this consequentialist line of argument.

Gay activists highlight the healthy, happy minority of gays as though their existence were evidence for the goodness of certain sorts of same-sex sexual activity. Few people, however, would regard the health and happiness of some racists as a demonstration of the moral legitimacy of racism. That

God may use human sin as the occasion for the communication of his grace (it goes too far to say that human sin is itself a "means of grace") is no justification of the sin.[132]

A second path, then, which may be followed from the judgement that sin is the embrace of death is this: even where healthy, happy lives are led by sinners, those lives are living deaths so far as sin is embraced. This is a statement of faith, which is to say it requires that God be true, though all human beings be liars, and it insists that visibility is not the sole criterion of truth. That homosexual sexual activity is biologically unproductive, physically dangerous, and often relationally destructive is unsurprising, but it is not these features which render it the embrace of death. It is, quite simply, the embrace of death because it is the defiance of the God who is life.

### Turning from God, disappointment, and frustration

Having turned from the source of life, how will the sinner live? The sexual promiscuity which is an astonishingly common (though not universal) characteristic of homosexual life is, quite simply, a restless search for life and love and truth which, like all idolatries, will result in continual disappointment:

> Be appalled, O heavens, at this, be shocked, be utterly desolate, says the LORD, for my people have committed two evils: they have forsaken me, the fountain of living water, and dug out cisterns for themselves, cracked cisterns that can hold no water. (Jer. 2:12–13)

### Toying with death

The embrace of death will, at its extremes, manifest itself in a deliberate toying with death. The love of risk, shown in many forms of sexual sin, is itself a defiance of authority – whether it is the statistical authority of death rates associated with particular behaviors or the social authority of well- or ill-informed public opinion. The incurve (the homosexual sinner as a person turned in on himself) has embraced true death in the turn from God. Now, at one and the same time, he seeks spiritual life outside of God *and* toys with physical and relational death. The search for a god who can secure and sustain the sinner's welfare will take him to the grave. Fallen sexuality, a radical disorientation, is a form of death. It is said of the strange woman, the adulteress of Proverbs, that,

> her way [house] leads down to death, and her paths to the shades;

> those who go to her never come back, nor do they regain the paths of life . . .

> Her feet go down to death; her steps follow the path to Sheol.

> She does not keep straight to the path of life. (Prov. 2:18–19, 5:5–6)

### The forms of life

This disorientation will apply not only to life as such but also to the *forms* of life as God has made it. Freedom, mutuality, order, embodiedness, health, fruitfulness, joy, and future-orientation are key features of the good life that God has given. The incurve inverts these forms of life. Foucault's is a "liberationist ideal of the body as open to the multiple possibilities of polymorphous perversity,"[133] yet life in sin is slavery and the desperate compulsions and addictions of Foucault's own life give the lie to this dimension of his faith: "They promise them freedom, but they themselves are slaves of corruption" (2 Pet. 2:19).

### Mutuality and order

As to mutuality, the implication of same-sex sexual activity, and perhaps this is more obviously true with some ideologically self-conscious lesbian radicals than with others, is that the "other" is not needed. Life under God is a recognition of dependence and an embrace of mutuality. Sin, conversely, is an assertion of independence and a longing for autonomy. As to order, sin is revolutionary, inverting the structure of reality so that the beast becomes ruler rather than ruled and his word, rather than God's, is believed and obeyed. Richard Hays, reflecting on why homosexual sexual activity should be the focus of attention in Romans 1, puts it like this:

> [Paul] singles out homosexual intercourse because . . . [it was] a particularly graphic image of the way in which human fallenness distorts God's created order.[134]

## Embodiment

Embodiment, or embodied-ness, is inescapable for the living human person. God's purposes for humans are that they know and serve God within the constraints of time and space. Sin, rebelling against these purposes, either endeavors to transcend this finitude or, in hatred of God, more commonly makes the body a substitute god. Hating his own body and worshipping the bodies of others, the sinner misdirects the use and thwarts the purpose of embodiment.

## Health, fruitfulness, and joy

Cautious still about "trading in stereotypes" or deploying utilitarian arguments, the case for the legitimacy of homogenital acts is, to say the least, unproven, if the appeal rests on other features of the good life which God gives such as health, fruitfulness, and joy. On the contrary, loneliness, rebellion for its own sake, desire to punish parents, self-pity, betrayal-pain and betrayal-anger, feelings of inadequacy, mistrust of others, the longing for and flight from intimacy and commitment, sadness, resentment, and low self-esteem are the characteristics of the sinner and, therefore, of the homosexual sinner as well.

## Future-orientation

Finally, the embrace of death manifests itself in the loss of future-orientation. Jenson comments that "Refusal of the future is self-destruction, and it therefore creates and sets free within us impulses and voices that counsel death."[135] James Jordan makes a similar point in a discussion of Genesis 4:17:

> After Cain murdered Abel and was driven out of the land of Eden, we read that he had a son whom he named Enoch, and that he founded a city that he also named Enoch (Genesis 4:17). The city, we are told, was named for his son. This was the first city ever built, but it will not be the last. The last city is the New Jerusalem, built by God the Father on the basis of the blood of God the Son through the power of God the Spirit, and "named" not for a son but for a Daughter: the Bride, Daughter Jerusalem. As Enoch was prince of the city of Enoch, so Christ is the Prince of the holy city.
>
> A city named for a son has no future, for femininity is eschatological. Man came first; then woman. Man after man after man after man is no future. The idea of a city's and a son's having the same name is ultimately narcissistic, which is the same as ultimately homosexual, for the son is married to himself, to a man. The true City of God is the Bride, married to the Son King.[136]

# Sin is the contradiction of love and the embrace of loathing

## Plurality is necessary for love

Sin is a rejection of God and is therefore the contradiction of love and the embrace of loathing. Commenting upon Genesis 1:26–27, Roy Clements writes,

> Looking back at this ancient text from a Christian perspective, it is tempting to speculate that a single human individual cannot fully reflect the complexity of God's likeness. Augustine long ago made this suggestion in his discussion of the doctrine of the Trinity. If love is an essential part of the divine being, he reasoned, then there must of necessity be Another who is the eternal object of that love. And if humankind is to "image" such a God, then inter-personal relationship must be intrinsic to our existence too.[137]

This statement raises two questions about fallen sexuality. The first relates to which criteria we are to apply in order to distinguish between true love and false. The second, more particularly relevant to discussions of homosexuality, relates to whether same-sex sexual activity can truly be regarded as engagement with "Another."

### True love

As to the first question, it is plain that the perfectly loving being and character of God will not contradict or be contradicted by his word of loving instruction, the law. The law is to love, and love fulfills the law (2 John 6; Rom. 13:8–10). If an attitude or action is lawless then, by definition, it is not loving. Since the law is the revelation of the God who is love in his character, authority, and purpose, transgression of the law cannot be loving. The Ramsay Colloquium puts it this way:

> We do not doubt that many gays and lesbians – perhaps especially those who seek the blessing of our religious communities – believe that theirs is the only form of love, understood as affection and erotic satisfaction, of which they are capable. Nor do we doubt that they have found in such relationships something of great personal significance, since even a distorted love retains traces of love's grandeur. Where there is love in morally

disordered relationships we do not censure the love. We censure the form in which that love seeks expression.[138]

It is for this reason that the argument for the legitimacy of homoerotic acts from their conformity to the double command to love God and love one's neighbor is superficial. If the double command is the summary of the law, then transgression of those laws that it summarizes will hardly qualify as obedience to the double command itself.[139]

## Love and lust

Robert Jenson expands upon this idea, reflecting upon Augustine:

> Augustine's description of his own career of lust remains unmatched. The principal passage is deservedly one of the most renowned in literature: "To Carthage then I came, and a welter of corrupted loves assaulted me from all sides. I was not yet in love; I was in love with being in love. With secret yearning I despised myself for not yearning enough. I searched for an object of love, loving to love." (*Confessions* iii.1) . . . The essence of Augustine's situation was that his love had first and foremost itself, and just so its own absence, for its object. He was "in love with being in love," he was "loving to love." As idolatry is worship hiddenly turned from God to the would-be worshipper, so lust is love hiddenly turned from the creaturely beloved to the would-be lover.[140]

True love, then, is love that reflects and is grounded in the love of God. We love rightly only so far as we love for, in, and because of God. But love that arises from God's loving character will be love shaped by God's loving purpose, which is expressed in the Torah. To love unlawfully is simply not to love. In Augustine's terms, it will be to lust. Jenson continues, "the crimes of desire forbidden by the commandments are immediate instances of lust: I cannot, for paradigmatic example, sexually love my neighbour's spouse, I can only lust after him or her."[141] The person I desire is a person in relation, and in desiring him or her contrary to his or her relations, I separate that person from his or her true self and person-hood and to that degree, I "depersonalize her or him, and just so create an object of lust."[142] Jenson concludes,

> The point is not psychological: I can of course sincerely long for and cherish my neighbour's spouse, also sexually, as can she or he me. What I cannot do is love her or him in the sense of the second "great commandment."[143]

## Loving the Other

Love in God is the giving of self to the other – hetero-donation. Although the Son is the image of the invisible God, he is not the same person but an Other. Father, Son, and Holy Spirit are identical as God and yet, having the same nature, they are not the same person. The Son is not the Father's Father, nor is the Father the Son's Son. And this means that their mutual self-giving is hetero-donation and not homo-donation. This is symbolized in marriage which is, by definition, heterosexual. The woman came from man, shared the nature of man (she, too, is in the image of God), and yet is different from man. God dealt with the not-goodness of aloneness by creating an Other rather than by replicating the one.[144] As the Ramsay Colloquium states:

> In the creative complementarity of male and female we are directed toward community with those unlike us. In the com-munity between male and female, we do not and cannot see in each other mere reflections of ourselves. In learning to appreci-ate this most basic difference, and in forming a marital bond, we take both difference and community seriously.[145]

Once more, Robert Jenson states this forthrightly,

> Homoerotic acts, however occasioned or motivated, constitute desertion in the face of the threatening other sort of human, defection from the burden of co-humanity. Therefore homo-eroticism is, in the present terms, always lust, and powerful attraction to it is a grievous affliction. That Scripture, on the rare occasions when the matter is mentioned, treats homoerotic acts as self-evidently sin, disaster, or both, is not an accident of Scripture's historical conditioning but follows directly from its whole understanding of human being.[146]

## Closed to God's love, we are loveless

Moreover, whereas God's fullness of life is infinite, humankind in creaturely finitude can only love with the love with which we are loved by God. And if the sinner is *homo se incurvatus*, or man turned in on himself, then, closed to the love of God, he is loveless. Afraid of giving to others and discovering self-emptiness the sinner, as sinner, is one who refuses to love in the giving of self to another. Rather than giving to the other in order to glorify and enhance the other, the sinner's primary relationship is with himself or what is most like him.

The form that this relationship takes appears to differ significantly between gay men on the one hand and lesbians on the other. Faced with the emptiness that results from turning from the love of God, gay men seek to fill the gap and lesbians to deny the gap. As to the first, Rich Bledsoe puts it this way:

> Hence the homosexual self seeks to cannibalize on other selves, to suck or absorb some hoped for beauty or perfection. Homosexuals do not seek to complement the incomplete self through erotic attachment to the opposite sex . . . they seek to reproduce or duplicate a hoped for ideal self using the other.[147]

By contrast, lesbianism, as radicalized feminism, denies the gap by the assertion of autonomy. Jerry Muller describes this phenomenon:

> The logic by which lesbianism is regarded as the truly authentic form of feminism was memorably spelled out by Charlotte Bunch in her article "Lesbians in Revolt," first published in 1972. "Heterosexuality separates women from each other," she wrote. "It makes women define themselves through men; it forces women to compete against each other for men and the privilege which comes through men and their social standing. . . Lesbianism is the key to liberation and only women who cut their ties to male privilege can be trusted to remain serious in the struggle against male dominance." The assertion that heterosexual masculinity is defined by the subordination of women has since become a mainstay of gay/lesbian theory. On this understanding, non-oppressive sexual relations are only possible between members of the same sex, and heterosexual women are victims of false consciousness, brainwashed into believing that their true interests lie in loving men rather than other women.
>
> The impact of this logic upon the lives of feminists has been palpable. "Lesbian feminism, by affirming the primacy of women's relationships with each other and by providing an alternative feminist culture, forced many nonlesbians to re-evaluate their relationships with men, male institutions, and male values," explains Estelle Freedman, a historian at Stanford. "In the process, feminists have put to rest the myth of female dependence on men and rediscovered the significance of female bonding."[148]

This clearly does not mean that there is *no* other-ness about another person of the same sex, nor that only love between man and woman can be called love, nor that only love capable of sexual expression with one sexually different is real love. It is, however, to take seriously the creation of male and female, as different, in the image of God. Humankind at its most fundamental is male-female. As Barth wrote, "The woman is for the man the eminent . . . co-human, and the man is this for the woman."[149]

## Sex as the final gesture

Additionally, it is to be recognized that sexual union is plainly the "gestural embodiment" of "the fullness and totality of . . . mutual commitment," which is to say that sexual self-giving is the nearest thing a human being can get to unconditional promise.[150] Thus, although this concept requires prior agreement with Gagnon's point that "the Bible presents the anatomical, sexual, and procreative complementarity of male and female as clear and convincing proof of God's will for sexual unions,"[151] the argument from fittingness is that heterosexual married love is the epitome or archetype of love of the other and the rejection of it undermines all other human loves.[152]

## Love of the father and gay men

Yet even though sexual love provides the final gesture, as summation of love, it is in the love of the father that life begins. A fallen nature, one disoriented from God, cannot believe and will not accept that God truly loves him. It is utterly unsurprising, therefore, that the incurve, and in particular the gay man, is almost invariably suffering from the "father wound." He has not learned from his father how to be a man. Starved of a father's love and angry with the father, the homosexual's life has a reparative drive that is fueled by excessive anger. When one turns from the love of God, there are only false solutions available – anti-sacraments, cannibalism, and murder. Compulsive, doomed, wicked, harmful, and tragic, the sinner seeks anywhere else than in God, the true Other, what can only be found in God. The frustration that results – the ambivalence of longing and anger, need and fear – leads to many forms of loathing. Hating God, the sinner hates his true self, made in the image of God. He hates all other human beings as well, but especially the threatening Other and the untrusted father.

### The embrace of loathing: the sinner as hater

Plainly, then, it is only in relationship with God in his fullness, trusting that God's love will not one day run dry, and only in the light of God's kindness, that the sinner can learn to love again.

> For we ourselves were once foolish, disobedient, led astray, slaves to various passions and pleasures, passing our days in malice and envy, despicable, hating one another. But when the goodness and loving kindness of God our Savior appeared, he saved us, not because of any works of righteousness that we had done, but according to his mercy, through the water of rebirth and renewal by the Holy Spirit. This Spirit he poured out on us richly through Jesus Christ our Savior, so that, having been justified by his grace, we might become heirs according to the hope of eternal life. The saying is sure. I desire that you insist on these things, so that those who have come to believe in God may be careful to devote themselves to good works; these things are excellent and profitable to everyone. (Titus 3:3–8)

The move from hating and being hated on the one hand, to being devoted to good works that profit others on the other, is a move possible only through the kindness of God. For God's saving action flows from his mercy, rather than depending upon our performance, and his fullness is ours in the pouring out of the Spirit, richly, by grace, giving hope of eternal life.[153]

*The love of God grounds self-giving*

It is the God-centeredness of this way of living as a human being which secures men and women for a life of giving to the other – whatever their sexual orientation and marital status. While it is true that the first object of self-giving for married persons is their spouse, it is the love of God which is the ground and content of that self-giving. Thus, in the absence of the spouse, the appetite of the renewed human being – which is, after all, an appetite to give in love to others rather than to take in desperation for self – does not go unmet. As C. S. Lewis put it:

> I take it for certain that the *physical* satisfaction of homosexual desires is sin. This leaves the [homosexual] no worse off than any normal person who is, for whatever reason, prevented from marrying.[154]

*Self-loathing narcissism*

It is, however, sadly true that the sinner's embrace of loathing, as we have seen, is not merely a loathing of God and of the other. It also extends to self-loathing. We may summarize our earlier reflections upon this. If we define "self" as the image of God in us, then outside of Christ we hate ourselves. If we define "self" as our identity as autonomous God-haters, then we love ourselves.[155] But God does not allow us to be fully consistent, and therefore we do not hate our image-of-God-self as totally and unreservedly as we otherwise would. And we do not love our autonomous-God-hater-self as totally and unreservedly as we otherwise would. We really are mixed up and messed up by sin. We both love and hate ourselves.

*Self-justification and blame*

Loving ourselves leads to self-justification and self-praise. If something is wrong with my life, then it must be somebody else's fault. Self-pity, a sense of victimhood, deep hurt, and a resentful resolve to blame others all combine in the sinner. The opening paragraph of Dostoyevsky's *Notes from the Underground* captures this powerfully:

> I am a sick man. . . I am a spiteful man. I am an unattractive man. I believe my liver is diseased. However, I know nothing at all about my disease, and do not know for certain what ails me. I don't consult a doctor for it, and never have, though I have a respect for medicine and doctors. Besides, I am extremely super-stitious, sufficiently so to respect medicine, anyway (I am well-educated enough not to be superstitious, but I am superstitious). No, I refuse to consult a doctor from spite. That you probably will not understand. Well, I understand it, though. Of course, I can't explain who it is precisely that I am mortifying in this case by my spite: I am perfectly well aware that I cannot "pay out" the doctors by not consulting them; I know better than anyone that by all this I am only injuring myself and no one else. But still, if I don't consult a doctor it is from spite. My liver is bad, well – let it get worse![156]

Here we have the typical incurved sinner, characterized by simultaneous narcissism and self-loathing and combining the desperate pursuit of pleasure and the bitter infliction of self-harm; sadness, anger, hurt, and a refusal to trust; longing for intimacy and simultaneously terrified of giving. All sinners are this way, homosexual and heterosexual sinners, radically disoriented and turned from God. Gollum, the pathetic crea-ture in Tolkien's *The Lord of the Rings* (so powerfully por-trayed in Peter Jackson's film version) captures this with power and pathos: the creature turned in on itself who weeps and rages by turns and is both untrustworthy in his malice and lust and yet desperately, desperately sad in his incurva-ture. Victim and culprit, tragic and wicked, simultaneously embracing and destroyed by the "precious" – that which must be exclusively his own and which prevents him opening up to the other. This, too, is the practicing homosexual. This, too, is every sinful human being.

The tragedy of the self-defeating sinner is clearer still when it is understood that there are only two ways of dealing with the pain of sin. The sinner can either submit to the death of the God-hating self ("whoever would save his life will lose it") or he can embrace more sin in a vain attempt to dull the pain which sin itself brings. The sinner loves the God-hating self and, apart from the sovereign and extraordinary grace of God, cannot bear the thought of that self's death. Yet to take the only alternative – more sin – is to choose another way of death that spirals down into ever deeper pain.

## Scapegoating, betrayal, psychic complexity

Rich Bledsoe, engaging with the thought of René Girard, has explored the form of self-justification that the self-loathing narcissist adopts.[157] In the "old world," the strong hero figure was an island of order in a world of chaos, a man of action who fought against the fates and against death. Where there was trouble the hero would externalize that trouble, allowing no internal division, self-doubt, or anxiety. This would entail the adoption of the scapegoating mechanism and thus the hero acted as a persecutor rivaling God by his use of power and keeping the balance of his soul through warfare. But in the cross of Christ, God has unmasked the scapegoat myth – for here is one who gives himself over to be persecuted and destroyed as the true Innocent.

Since Calvary, then, the God whom the sinner rivals is seen as the weak one, the suffering servant. Thus sinful rivalry of God now takes the form of victimhood, of being one of the persecuted. So, in the modern world, the persecutor is the one who presents himself as a victim, and persecution is prosecuted through victimhood. The sinner causes himself to stumble, blames others, and really believes the accusations he makes against them. Meanwhile, his victimhood is a focus upon his own hurt and despair. The sinner therefore experiences "psychic complexity," misery, anxiety, self-pity, and neurosis. The incurve, the radically disoriented sinner, and, not least, the practicing homosexual, regards himself as the misunderstood outcast who dies for others, the counterfeit Wounded Healer.[158]

Bledsoe goes on to describe the sense of betrayal which lies at the heart of the modern victim-sinner. So far as he still sees and, indeed, believes something of the truth of God, the sinner knows that God is right and that he, the sinner, deserves to die. The choice is simple and awful: to die with Christ, putting to death the self-as-God-hater; or to die some other way, by persecuting the self-as-God-lover.[159] The human person is not big enough for these two selves to coexist permanently, and the neurosis of the sinner is the psychic masochism of hurting one self or the other. Apart from the work of God the Holy Spirit, therefore, the incurve's choice will be to "embrace a thousand other agonies in order to avoid the one agony of dying with Jesus."[160]

## Sin is the contradiction of truth and the embrace of falsehood

Sin is a rejection of God and is therefore the contradiction of truth and the embrace of falsehood. As Hilary of Poitiers said,

> Our disbelief tilts even against obvious truth; we strive in our fury to pluck even God from His throne. If we could, we would climb by bodily strength to heaven, would fling into confusion the ordered courses of sun and stars, would disarrange the ebb and flow of tides, check rivers at their source or make their

waters flow backward, would shake the foundations of the world, in the utter irreverence of our rage against the paternal work of God. It is well that our bodily limitations confine us within more modest bounds. Assuredly, there is no concealment of the mischief we would do if we could. In one respect we are free; and so with blasphemous insolence we distort the truth and turn our weapons against the words of God.[161]

The ways in which sinners "distort the truth" are manifold.

## Sin as madness

Sin is, first of all, a variety of madness.

The line between such sin and what we have been taught to call mental illness is indefinite and porous, if indeed it obtains at all . . . Rationality is not a capacity, it is rather a virtue; and irrationality is not an incapacity but a sin, of despair.[162]

God is the reality who surrounds us and defines us and surrounds and defines nature and history. He is the ultimate reality. Thus sin, which is a rejection of and a flight from him, is a rejection of and a flight from reality. Discrepancy between the world in our heads and the world outside of our heads is an error, a lie, or madness. To live by that discrepancy is to live out of touch with reality, in an unreal and untrue world, and to think that we advance ourselves by disobeying God.

## Sin as stupidity

Second, the embrace of falsehood that the rejection of God involves initiates a spiral of ignorance from simple ignorance to studied ignorance to stupefied and stupefying ignorance. Just as sin is its own anti-reward, so the sinner's view of sin is self-reinforcing. The last thing the sinner does – as sinner – is to challenge his own views of his sins. Self-deception and partial moral sensibility characterize all sinners. Hypocrisy runs deep in us all. All this can be seen in a variety of ways in relation to homosexual activity. The refusal of those engaging in such activity to pay attention to the likely consequences, assuming that the probabilities or averages do not apply in their case, is a widespread denial of reality. The homophobe's blindness of spirit leads him to a hypocrisy that is no less serious, as he bitterly condemns the sins of others.

Likewise, the twists and tangles of those who wish simultaneously to uphold biblical authority and the legitimacy of some same-sex sexual activity are hard to fathom. Wolfhart Pannenberg summarizes:

> Thus, the entire biblical witness includes practicing homosexuality without exception among the kinds of behavior that give particularly striking expression to humanity's turning away from God. This exegetical result places very narrow boundaries around the view of homosexuality in any church that is under the authority of Scripture.[163]

Richard B. Hays is equally forthright:

> The fact is that Paul treats *all* homosexual activity as *prima facie* evidence of humanity's tragic confusion and alienation from God the Creator . . . Though only a few biblical texts speak of homoerotic activity, all that do mention it express unqualified disapproval.[164]

Because the biblical text is so clear, a survey of reactions to John Boswell's work produces assessments such as "a textbook case of reading into the text what one wants to find there" (Richard Hays), "influential but highly misleading"

(David Wright), "advocacy scholarship" and "historical learning yoked to a cause, scholarship in the service of a social and political agenda" (Robert Wilken).[165] It is sad, but unsurprising, that Robert Jenson concludes, "The most sophisticated defenses against the mandate of rationality . . . are those thrown up by seemingly radical obedience to it."[166]

## Rhetoric at the service of self-justification

Thirdly, the embrace of falsehood fuels the quest for self-justification, as mentioned above. All sinners show an inventiveness and persistence in devising deflections, distractions, smoke screens, and excuses in order to avoid or escape condemnation for sin. It comes as no surprise, therefore, that this is the case in regard to the propaganda of gay activism. Recurring rhetorical devices include accusing opponents of a related sin (homophobia, minority-hatred, and control-obsession); making a virtue of vice ("we're guilty of love"); explaining problems associated with a particular sin as the consequences of opposition to that sin (the issue of "internalized homophobia"); pressing positive vocabulary into the service of sin ("gay," "intergenerational intimacy"); and endeavoring to connect the relevant behavior with values which appeal in the cultural climate (homosexuals as more intimate, creative, enlightened, and individuated; homosexual partnerships as more loving and faithful than heterosexual partnerships).[167]

On this last point, Satinover speaks of the "supernormalizing" of homosexuals – following the trajectory of ways in which the perception of homosexuality has progressed from sin-crime, to disease-misfortune, to anomaly (aberration), to minority normality (lifestyle choice). Supernormalizing makes an ideal of homosexual relationships, and only apotheosis remains! On the wider point, David Selbourne[168] is one of many to protest that moral argument is, in much contemporary debate, giving way to moral evasion.[169]

## Mistaken identity

All sinners reinvent themselves. Uncomfortable with and dismissive of their entry in God's dictionary, they construct their own redefinition. Joseph Nicolosi says simply, "The homosexual has not so much a sexual problem as an identity problem."[170] Since identity, a sense of who we are and of what makes us who we are, is one of the primary "logical levels" at which specifically human consciousness begins, it becomes the battleground for spiritual forces and culture warriors alike.

## Confusing logical levels

A widely understood device of gay activism, therefore, has been the deliberate confusion of what some call "logical levels."[171] At its simplest, it is a mistake to confuse a single behavior with a capability ("I hit par on the tenth hole" with "I play to scratch"), let alone a repeated behavior with an identity ("I eat cornflakes every day" with "being a cornflake-eater defines the person I am"). Yet gay propaganda has the effect of encouraging those with a homosexual orientation to "draw identity from their sexuality and thus to shift the ground of their identity subtly and idolatrously away from God."[172]

This is not altogether misconstrued. The work of experts such as Elizabeth Moberley, Richard Fitzgibbons, and Joseph Nicolosi, for example, suggests that a significant element in the inculcation of homosexual orientation in men is the development of identity problems in early life. All of them focus upon the search for the lost masculine self, the father-wound, and identity confusion which result from "defensive detachment from the disappointing father," a mistrust of relationship with women as exhausting and draining, and the addictive disorders which arise from the reparative drive in abused and hurting individuals.[173]

## Self-reinvention

This process is not, however, always or altogether unconscious. The sinner refuses or flees from the authentic identity of embracing life, love, and truth in the perfect person and purpose of God and instead sets about the task of self-reinvention. This is part of an essentially existential ethical relativism that insists upon the autonomy of the individual human person in the definition of humanness. Foucault's constructivism gave him grounds, he thought, to hope for changes in society's attitudes to sexual orientation and behavior. "By revealing, [through his study of the history of sexuality] that ideas about sex are human creations, he hoped to neutralize their power and pave the way for emancipation."[174] Beyond this, the importance of a plasticity of identity may form one level of explanation of the complex phenomenon of the love of gay men for theater. As Oscar Wilde put it, "Naturalness is just another pose."[175] Samuel Johnson said that "He who makes a beast of himself gets rid of the pain of being a man."[176]

Joseph Nicolosi explains that

> Gay identity is not "discovered" as if it existed *a priori* as a natural trait. Rather it is a culturally approved process of *self-reinvention* by a group of people in order to mask their collective emotional hurts.[177]

## Community, identity, and the failure of the church

This last phrase, "collective emotional hurts," is crucial. All sinners selectively connive at the sins of others. We enter into a multitude of unwritten and usually unspoken contracts with other sinners, and the terms are simple: "you keep silent about, rationalize, condone or approve my sin, and I will do the same for yours." This contract only ever becomes explicit among a persecuted group which, by virtue of being persecuted for its behaviors, has no choice but to "speak its name." But when it does speak its name it must do so in terms of approval: it is the "love" which now must fight its corner. The words that are spoken are words celebrating the sinful behavior and expressing hatred of those who disapprove. The readiness to shock or to fight those who disapprove is greatly increased when, in whatever way, the individual has come to believe that his membership in this disapproved group defines him or is the most important thing about him.

It is not that other groups may not unconsciously contribute to this process. The pretense of sexually fallen heterosexuals within the church that all is well with them is a comforting lie. The deep, deep failure of the church to believe that temptation to homosexual sin is not sin has made it almost impossible for those confused about or troubled by their sexual orientation to speak honestly or seek counsel. And when one community offers neither understanding nor help in resolving identity pain, it is not surprising that those seeking such help will seek an alternative community.

With all of this, though, Richard Hays is right to assert that "never within the canonical perspective does sexuality become the basis for defining a person's identity or for finding meaning and fulfilment in life."[178] Part of the sinner's flight from his identity as a creature known by God and possessing God-given purpose is to insist that there are other (more important) bases for identity. Views of sex in the modern world reveal a peculiar mix of the exaggerated and the trivialized. Hays reminds us that in the biblical view, "freedom, joy and service are possible without sexual relations."[179] No other view can account for the sexual moral perfection and complete human integrity of Jesus of Nazareth, the way, the truth, and the life.

# Conclusion

Sin is theologically defined, deicidal, and suicidal. As the rejection of the God who is life, love, and truth, sin is the embrace of death, loathing, and falsehood. If exploration of these themes is put beside observation of a particular set of behaviors and there is a fit between them, then that constitutes an argument *ex convenientia* that such behaviors are sinful. Thus the themes explored in this chapter serve to reinforce the conclusions of exegetes, medical practitioners, social psychologists, and others that same-sex sexual activity falls short of God's purpose that humankind should reflect his life, love, and truth. It is thereby seen to be sinful. At the same time, since "all have sinned and fall short of the glory of God," none are exempt from the responsibility to reflect upon the contours and trajectories of sin and to consider the bankruptcy of all remedies for it which do not have their source in God.

If sinners are disoriented, then they need reorientation. If their lives are characterized by death, loathing, and falsehood, then only the life, love, and truth of God can set them free. If they are divided, broken, and self-alienated, then only Christ, torn apart and broken in their place, can restore them to God and to integrity. If they are self-loathing narcissists, then only the breath of the Spirit can replace hatred with love and self-obsession with adoration of God. Sin goes deep. It is complex and painful, tragic and wicked. Grace alone can reach the sinner, and love alone can win.

# 5

# Radical Disorientation

## Fallen Sexuality and the Christian Doctrine of Sin (II)

### David Field

At the broadest level all humans are heirs to a predisposition that we have not chosen and that propels us towards self-destruction and evil – our sinful nature . . . We all face the same challenge: how are we to live when what we want is out of accord with what God tells us we should want in this life?[180]

## Introduction

In Chapter 4 we saw that what we know theologically to be true about sin will necessarily illumine our understanding of particular sinful behaviors and that, conversely, careful reflection upon particular sinful behaviors will confirm and refine our doctrine of sin. We saw this as we explored sin as theologically defined, deicidal, and suicidal. We also saw that, as the rejection of God who is life, love, and truth, sin is the embrace of death, loathing, and falsehood. Of particular importance in considering the sins of same-sex sexual activity is the relationship between orientation and behavior. This chapter provides helpful insight into this vital matter by applying the theological truth of the equal ultimacy of the one and the many in God. If God is one and many, and sin is theologically defined, then sin, too, will be one and many. This truth has both theological and pastoral significance and underlines the fact that since sin is a God-problem, it is amenable only to a God-solution.

## The "one and the many" and the Triune God

The work of the Dutch-American theologian Cornelius Van Til in the middle of the twentieth century highlighted, as never before, the axiomatic status of the Christian assertion of the equal ultimacy of the one and the many in the triune being of God and its importance for Christian epistemology. In the triunity of God alone is there resolution of the philosophical problem of the one and the many.[181] The search for unifying and ordering principles in a world of particulars and change is hopeless without the three and one Creator God. Creation is one because God made it and purposefully governs it. Creation is many because God made it and purposefully governs it. And so with the activity of human persons made in the image of God we have not merely the unity of actor and multiplicity of effects, but even in the effects themselves a oneness and multiplicity. All objects, events, and persons in the world are under the sovereign government and authoritative interpretation of God. Each and every object, event, and person is related to each and every other object, event, and person in and through the one sovereign triune God.

## Sin is one and many

For this reason, each and every sin and sinner is related to each and every other sin and sinner and yet, because they are all under the sovereign rule and purposeful understanding of God, each and every sin and sinner is distinct from each and every other sin and sinner. The answer, then, to the compound question, "Is sin one or many?" is "Yes!" Sin is one, although committed by billions of human agents in an almost infinite variety of situations, because sin is always an assault upon the holy character, sovereign authority, and loving purpose of the one God. Sin is many, even though invariably characterized by the assault upon the one God, because it is the work of innumerable moral agents, no two of whom are ever in precisely the same situation (moment and location, to take but two features). The singleness of sin derives from the oneness of the God against whose perfection it is directed and its multiplicity flows from the particularities of his creation in time and space which ensures that no two manifestations of rebellion against him are identical.

## A taxonomy of sin

This concept is important when we take up the task of producing a taxonomy of sin. Since all objects in creation are made by and reveal the one God, they all can also reveal something of each other – if only we have the wisdom, purity, and mental capacity to discern this. God compares himself to a moth, a lion, and a rock, and although we know that moths, lions, and rocks are separate and distinct, we also know that they are related as revelations of God. Every thing is related to and tells us about every other thing, even while every thing is distinct and separate from every other thing. So it is with sin. Every single sin is like and unlike every other single sin. Each and every sin tells us something, but not everything, about each and every other sin. Each and every sin is an image or a symbol of each and every other sin. Each and every sin provides a perspective on each and every other sin. We will only fully know one sin by knowing all others.[182] In some respects all sins are alike, or one. In other respects all sins are unlike, or many.

## All sins alike and unlike: three illustrations

Three illustrations will help to clarify this concept. First, in at least one sense, to be guilty of one sin is to be guilty of all. On one level this is simply because all sins are against the same person, the holy Creator God.

> Whoever keeps the whole law but fails in one point has become accountable for all of it. For the one who said, "You shall not commit adultery," also said, "You shall not murder." Now if you do not commit adultery but if you murder, you have become a transgressor of the law. (Jas. 2:10–11)

Beyond this, however, comes the recognition that all sinners are engaged in the same project, or battle. The mob of rebels against God may carry a variety of weapons, but they are all rushing in the same direction with the same hostile demeanor and destructive intent. All sins are related to and thus, in a sense, bound up in, all others.

Second, the Scriptures tell us that in Jesus we have a high priest "who in every respect has been tested as we are, yet without sin" (Heb. 4:15). Whether we regard the temptations that Jesus experienced as single, threefold, or manifold, it is clear that they did not extend to every particular of the temptations of his people. Yet because sin is one and many, it can be said that he was tempted "in every respect."

Third, the Ten Commandments illustrate the truth that sin is one and many. One God gives ten distinct and separate

commands to the one redeemed people, who will live in different places at different times and face various temptations.
Because all sins are unlike, none of these commandments
will ever be broken in precisely the same way twice. Because
all sins are like, (a mere) ten commandments suffice to cover
all sins. Indeed, these Ten Commandments give different perspectives upon the same evil. The fall of Adam is a transgression of each of the ten commands. Adam's sin involved
putting other gods before God, bowing down in worship to
an image of God (the serpent), taking God's name in vain,
Sabbath-breaking, parent dishonoring, murder, adultery,
theft, false witness, and covetousness. Since sin is suicidal,
the Ten Commandments may be seen as ten commands to
embrace life or as ten prohibitions against particularly cruel
forms of self-harm.

Further, since sin is not only the root of human problems
but also a false attempt to "solve" our problems by attaining
perfection apart from God, the Ten Commandments may be
understood as prohibitions against false solutions to the
human predicament. The sinner is in pain and thinks that
worshipping other gods will heal his pain. In the first commandment, God says "no." The sinner thinks that his parents
are the problem and that dishonoring them will heal him. In
the fifth commandment, God says "no." The sinner thinks
that another person is the problem and that if this other person were murdered then all would be well, or that his wife is
the problem and that taking another woman is the solution.
In the sixth and seventh commandments, God says "no." The
situation is the same, of course, with idol worship, blas-
phemy, Sabbath-breaking, theft, false witness, and coveting.

### *"Families" or "classes" of sin*

It is possible, from the Ten Commandments, to make generalizations about sin that pull back from the ultimate

differentiation of sin as many and yet move on from the ultimate commonality of sin as one. There may be clusters of
sins that cut across sectors of human activity and range up
and down the being-to-doing spectrum (see Fig. 5.1, below).
Yet the sins which form these clusters, although each of them
is unique, have between them a commonality which warrants
studying them as a group. Because all sin is one, we need to
see, for example, that murder involves a lie in order to understand it properly. This lie is about what is good and valuable,
about what should be done away with, about how problems
are solved, about God's good intention for the murderer during the time he was committing the murder, and so on. To
understand a lie properly we will need to explore the relationship between truth and life, and it will not be long before
we conclude that the lie is, one way or another, an assault
upon life itself. But a lie is not fully or solely murder; nor is
murder fully or solely a lie. There is a family, or class, of sins
that may be called lying, and even though that class of sins
may overlap with and shed light upon murder, it is not the
same thing as the class of sins called murder.

## Sin is one and many: a representation and some implications

Figure 5.1, next page, illustrates the differences and similari-
ties between many of these classes of sins.

A      The fundamental orientation of the human person is
       either towards God or away from God.
B–B    At the deepest level of the sinner (top), what could be
       called his fallen nature, all sin is undifferentiated: it is
       one. At the level of single acts, thoughts, and words
       (bottom), all sin is differentiated. No one sin is the
       same as any other one sin: sin is many.

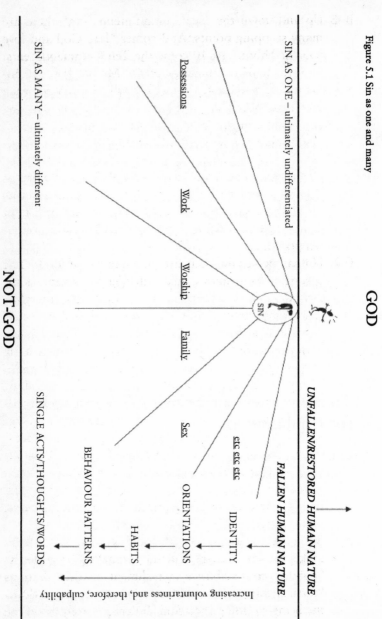

Figure 5.1 Sin as one and many

B–B  Up and down the "scale of differentiation" there are many stopping points. At 2 comes "love God and love your neighbor." At 10 come the Ten Commandments; at 613, the 613 commands of the Mosaic law; at ultimate differentiation, the perfect will of God for each and every single act, thought, and word of each and every single human being throughout history.

C    Human life can be regarded as being composed of various sectors.

D    Every person born in Adam (and all but one born of Adam) is born with a fallen human nature. The defilement and corruption of this nature render the sinner hostile to God, unable to please him and vulnerable to temptation.

E–E  Human beings live their lives at a number of levels. The spectrum from nature, through identity, orientations, attitudes and values, and habits to single acts, thoughts, and words is in no way intended as a precise description but merely as broad categories for these different levels

E–E  This spectrum can also be described as a being-doing continuum. Nature, identity, orientations, and attitudes and values go deep and represent what we are; habits, behavior patterns and single acts, thoughts, and words are nearer to the surface of human life and represent what we do. While the teaching of Scripture is that what we do flows from what we are (Matt. 12:33–37; 15:18–20), there is also a feedback loop in place so that particular choices at the level of acts, thoughts, and words reinforce and strengthen habits, orientations, and identity.

E–E  So far as the axiom of moral theology that "consent makes the sin" is correct, actual culpability (regarded as "liability to retributive punishment" rather than as "intrinsically moral evil") increases as one moves down the being-to-doing spectrum. Where precisely upon the

bottom horizontal a sinner sins is at a high level of vol-
untariness, whereas sins of orientation and identity
tend to be far less voluntary.

## Clusters of sins

Taking into account levels of orientation, identity, and attitudes and values, we may arrive at fresh taxonomies of sin in
each culture and generation. The concept of racism may be
used to illustrate. "Racism" may refer to attitudes, predispositions, innocent mistakes, violent behaviors, personal hurts,
group affiliations, and much more besides. Is the "racist" identified by what he believes, by what he does, by the groups he
belongs to, or by some other way? Is his racism genetically
determined or influenced? Or is it a social construct? Can he be
educated or medicated out of it? To ask these questions is to
indicate the huge potential for category errors if we carelessly
apply a single label to various levels of human personhood and
experience. It is also to indicate that there may be a real inter-
connectedness between a whole range of such phenomena.

Is it possible to apply the term "racism" to a cluster of
related human phenomena, some of which will be actively
sinful, others of which will be corrupt, though unchosen,
predispositions to particular sins, and others of which will
not be sinful at all? Will we not find in such a cluster a whole
range of desires, tastes, associations, preferences, perspectives, longings, aspirations, pains, resentments, resistances,
creativities, self-understandings, physical acts, political
activisms, forms of friendship, and attitudes to God? Is it
possible that "racism" may refer to a state, a stance, or a set
of actions? Indeed, is it possible that the culture, structure,
policies, and practices of an organization may so inculcate
and reward racist behaviors that we could declare it to be
"institutionally racist"? Surely that is possible.

## The total racist cannot exist

It is clear, however, that there will be no single person in whom all possible manifestations of racism will be found. In some, racism will be a full-blown, life-shaping power that determines almost all that is most important to them. Their self-identity, use of time, hopes, fears, passions, and choices of particular physical activities (violence against those of other "races") will all embody and express their racism. In others, racism may be an underlying and almost undetectable set of attitudes which conflict with their consciously held beliefs and preferences and which, the moment they surface in conscious thoughts or suggestions to act in a certain way, are immediately and vigorously rejected. How easy and how likely that rejection is may be heavily influenced by parental, peer-group, media-expressed, and societal attitudes – as well as by whether or not the law of the land encourages, allows, or prohibits the actions thus suggested. Finally, others still may choose to engage in violence against other ethnic groups and in chanting of racial abuse – not because they themselves have a racist orientation or hold racist attitudes, but solely as the deliberate choice of evil action for its own sake.

## Homosexuality is a cluster

It seems clear that, for all its imprecision, of which more below, "homosexuality" qualifies as such a family or cluster of sins. It may be better called by another name, and some have suggested "homosexualism." Or, taking a lead from the medieval description of the sinner as a person turned in on himself, *homo se incurvatus,* perhaps this cluster is the Incurve, or Incurvature? Whatever the label, the cluster itself will comprise a whole family of human attitudes and activities, which tend toward and find sinful expression in homosexual sexual behaviors. It will include all of those levels and manifestations suggested above: desires, tastes, associations, preferences, perspectives, longings, aspirations, pains, resentments, resistances, creativities, self-understandings, physical acts, political activisms, forms of friendship, and attitudes to God.

## A total Incurve cannot exist

No one human being will possess or express every manifestation of incurvature, and indeed, some manifestations may be mutually exclusive. But the Incurve is the hypothetical personification of the state of being and the set of values and attitudes, the orientation, desires, behaviors, and mores which find their defining, though not necessarily constitutive, expression in homosexual sexual activity. Because all sins are related, all sinners will participate in the Incurve. Because no two sins are the same, we will never find a single person who is and does everything we mean by Incurvature. The particular form of the hatred of God found in the Incurve will vary from the particular form found in the Racist, the Glutton, the Proud, the Angry, the Sluggard.[183] Each family of sins will embrace death, hatred, and falsehood in different ways. Yet, as families of sinners with particular sins as heads of household, all will reject God. All will therefore embrace death, hatred, and falsehood in place of the life, love, and truth that are in God.

# Two vital qualifications

## Sin is many, so there is no one such thing as "homosexuality"

Two qualifications must be made immediately, and they flow simply from the recognition that sin is many and sin is one.

First, the construction and deployment of an extrabiblical category like "homosexuality" or "the Incurve" forces the data and treats as unitary a wide and complex range of human phenomena (identity, beliefs and values, addictions, choices, social preferences, sexual activities). It thus fails to address what is and what is not sin, let alone to distinguish between the guilt, the corruption, and the inability of sin, or between the tragedy, the folly, and the wickedness of sin. As with all generalizations, great care is in order. The need for this qualification is widely recognized. As S. Joel Garver says,

> It is plainly false to assume that "homosexuality" or "being gay," on the psychological, emotional, and experiential level, is some kind of unified phenomenon either within our own time and culture or over time and among cultures. Sexuality is something that always comes to expression within a particular symbolic, ritual, social, and religious matrix. Thus across times and cultures, there is not a single thing that we can call "homosexuality" as we use that term today in a psychological sense, referring to a particular "orientation," even if analogies can be properly drawn. While we can still call sin "sin" in terms of particular behaviors, desires, life-patterns, and the like, an overly simplistic sexual taxonomy can be problematic, pastorally and therapeutically.[184]

For this reason, some propose simply talking about "homosexualities" because, as another writer puts it,

> "Homosexuality" obscures a complex set of mental, emotional and behavioral states caused by differing proportions of distinct influences, resulting in a broad spectrum of only loosely related outcomes.[185]

Of course, not only has the "historical and social manifestation of homosexuality" exhibited great diversity and differentiation,[186] but an accepted definition of sexuality or of what constitutes the sexual appears beyond reach too.[187]

### Sin is one, so all participate in the Incurve

The second qualification lies in precisely the opposite direction. Since all sin is one, in some ways and some measures all sinners will participate in the Incurve; all will be guilty of sins of homosexuality. It is not merely that "no-one is exempt from sexual brokenness";[188] it is also that the key sinful attitudes and orientations of homosexual sinners will manifest themselves sinfully in "non-homosexual" sinners too. Or, from one perspective, all sin is homosexual sin – just as from other perspectives all sin is murder, all sin is Sabbath-breaking, all sin is lying, and so on.

## Sin as one and many: practical implications for attitude change

### Inordinate horror at sin?

The unity, or alikeness, of sin means that there is such a thing as "inordinate" horror of particular sins. All human beings are capable of all possible sins, given the opportunity. For various reasons involving the mysterious sovereignty of God, who may use genetic coding, neurological structures, early life experiences, chemical imbalances, societal reinforcement, and any number of other secondary causes, one person is characterized by one set of disorientations while another person is characterized by a different set of disorientations. That is to say, that as the revolting mass of the human race charges down the main street of God's world seeking ways of defacing that world and defying its Maker, some will find pitchforks to use, others clubs, and still others swords. For the sword-wielding rebels to despise or profess disgust at those who carry pitchforks would be laughable were not the whole rabble under fearsome judgement. It has been remarked upon often enough that Romans 2 follows Romans 1, and the self-righteous homophobe falls as deeply under the wrath of God as those who engage in and justify same-sex sexual activity:

> Therefore you have no excuse, whoever you are, when you judge others; for in passing judgement on another you condemn yourself, because you, the judge, are doing the very same things. (Rom. 2:1)

Does the self-appointed judge practice the very same things, the self-same shameful sexual sins? Yes and no. Preaching against stealing, they steal; saying that one must not commit adultery, they commit adultery; abhorring idols, they rob temples. They do so not in exactly the same ways but as those characterized both by the same sinful inclinations and by the embrace of such activities as those inclinations lead to. Although it is the clear teaching of Scripture that some sins are more heinous than others, it is a false conclusion that one sinner is thereby given the right or the duty of hating the sins of others more than he hates his own (Matt. 11:21–24; Mark 3:28–30; Luke 12:47–48; John 19:11; 1 John 5:16–17).

But equally, an unspoken agreement between sinners to condone or to smile upon each other's rebellion would be no more than honor among thieves. All sins are utterly foul. Paul Jewett records the words spoken by the judge who pronounced sentence on Oscar Wilde:

> Oscar Wilde and Alfred Taylor, the crime of which you have been convicted is so bad that one has to put stern restraint upon one's self to protect one's self from describing, in language which I would rather not use, the sentiments which rise to the breast of every man of honour who has heard the details of

these two terrible trials . . . It is no use for me to address you.
People who can do these things must be dead to all sense of
shame, and one cannot hope to produce any effect upon them.[189]

Jewett goes on to comment that "Such an attitude of
loathing gay people is wholly without warrant in Scripture."
And Jewett is entirely wrong so to conclude. The attitude
expressed by the judge's words is fully appropriate in relation
to same-sex sexual activity. The problem arises when that
self-same attitude is not found in regard to any and every
other sin, too. The Christian believer, in his right mind, will
gladly take these words upon his lips with reference to his
own sin and will feel about himself precisely what the judge
felt about Oscar Wilde and Alfred Taylor.

Inordinate horror at sin, then, is not excessive horror – for
no horror at sin can be excessive. It is, rather, the horror that
discriminates in my favor and others' disfavor, which excuses
my sins while condemning the sins of others, which arises
from pride, fear, and unrighteous anger. It is horror that is not
horror at the sinfulness of an action, but at its strangeness. It
is the horror of offended taste rather than offended holiness.
This is particularly pertinent in matters of sexuality. Sadly,
many of those of a conservative theological or social stance
who assert an abhorrence of same-sex sexual activity regard
the adulterous behavior of the rich and famous, or the adulterous imaginations and fantasies of their own minds, with
casualness bordering on indifference.

### All sin in every direction
A sound instinct would suggest that all sinners are disoriented in their fallenness in regard to each of the dimensions of
life. As Robert Jenson has said,

> Sin is idolatry. We are sinners in that we revolve in our own self-
> reference and do so piously . . . Sin is lust. We are sinners in that

we refuse to grow up toward love . . . Sin is injustice. We are sinners in that we oppress and subserve one another, in that we
parry the demands of community . . . Sin is despair. We are sinners in that we take no risks.[190]

*Sexual sin pervasive*
Given the depth and inescapability of our sexual identity, it
would be unsurprising if human fallenness did not also manifest itself in sexual perversion in each of these dimensions of
life, making a god of sexual fulfillment (idolatry); regarding
others as objects of my sexual gratification (lust); relating to
others improperly and failing to give them their due – which
is loving and self-giving fidelity to my spouse and chastity to
all others (injustice); and unbelievingly refusing the risk
which serving others entails (despair). This being the case,
the inordinate horror at the sinful sexual activity of others
which is common in the church, expressed at both the individual and institutional level, is simultaneously ridiculous
and an aggravation of our own sexual sin.

# The orientation-behavior distinction

## Defining orientation

At this point it is necessary to give some attention to the
widely-used distinction between orientation and behavior
– first by way of description, and then by way of evaluation. The concept of sexual orientation is itself a slippery
one. One Christian writer describes homosexual orientation as "preferential erotic attraction to people of the same
sex" while recognizing that "sexual orientation does not
always correlate with sexual behavior."[191] David Matzgo
McCarthy, on the other hand, defines orientation much
more broadly:

> Orientation is not simply a matter of attraction or tendency
> toward a particular object of desire . . . It names a structure of
> interpersonal possibilities . . . Orientation is not entirely distinct
> from desires or acts, but it is superficial to refer to a homosexu-
> al orientation as merely a tendency of object-attraction. An ori-
> entation can be expressed in a multiplicity of different desires
> and acts, some explicitly sexual and others more akin to friend-
> ship, some temperate and others undisciplined, some superficial
> and others deeply expressive.[192]

Certainly it is not possible to apply the distinction with precision. A person may possess homosexual orientation
without engaging in homosexual sexual activity. Others will
engage in homoerotic acts without being oriented psycho-
logically toward same-sex attachment.

Much of the relevant literature also notes that the
concept of orientation is a relatively recent phenomenon.
Hays writes, "neither Paul nor anyone else in antiquity had a
concept of 'sexual orientation.'"[193] And Foucault summarizes,

> As defined by the ancient civil or canonical codes, sodomy was
> a category of forbidden acts; their perpetrator was nothing
> more than the juridical subject of them. The nineteenth-century
> homosexual became a personage, a past, a case history, and a
> childhood, in addition to being a type of life, a life form, and a
> morphology.[194]

### Legitimacy and use of the orientation-behavior distinction

The fundamental legitimacy of the distinction between orientation and behavior in relation to homosexuality is
grounded in the clear biblical rejection of certain sexual
behaviors, alongside an apparent silence regarding what we

would understand as homosexual orientation – and this in spite of the strong biblical emphasis on the root and source of sin being in the sinner's heart.

Christian use of the distinction has taken several forms. First, the lack of recognition of the distinction led to the confusion of temptation and sin. A certain person may have a powerful same-sex sexual attraction and thus a stronger temptation to engage in sinful sexual activity. This inclination is not, in itself, something for which they are culpable. But if the orientation-behavior distinction is not recognized, then the frequency or intensity of temptation's assault upon an individual could be seen as an indication of their deeper sinfulness. Second, the recognition of the distinction, which resulted in part from an awakening to sexual realities through twentieth-century research, led to greater hermeneutical and interpersonal maturity. Third, the distinction is, at times, almost overdrawn – as though digital rather than analogue – and the biblical condemnation of homosexual activity is read as though the issue of orientation were almost an irrelevance.[195]

This over-enthusiastic deployment of the orientation-behavior distinction may mask the extent to which states and stances are themselves "configurations of corruption," which may have a family resemblance with, or incline an individual to, particular sinful activities. Finally, if orientation is misread as voluntary preference, rather than as involuntary and deep-seated predisposition, then the usefulness of the distinction is lost because, in effect, orientation understood this way is back among the lustful desires which are in themselves sinful.

Debate over the origins and causes of homosexual orientation proceeds with pace and volume. Satinover summarizes recent research by saying that "like all other complex behavioral and mental conditions, homosexuality is multifactorial."[196]

# The orientation-behavior distinction: some theological considerations

A theological evaluation of the orientation-behavior distinction falls under six headings.

## The distinction derives from the fact that sin is one and many

Firstly, the orientation-behavior distinction itself correlates to sin as one and sin as many. This is clear from Figure 5.1, above. The ultimate commonality of sinners is found in their universal possession of a fallen sinful nature, a disorientation from God (Fig. 5.1 represents this by the sinner facing "not-God"). This inherited corruption or depravity is a predisposition or orientation that functions as a fount of evil inclinations, desires, and passions. It is a state or a stance, and yet it tends to fruition in actions and behaviors. It may arise from the actions of others and yet become a deepseated part of who we are. It can have no place in the new heavens and the new earth and yet, as we shall see, it has a definite though mysterious place in God's wise and loving dealings with us here and now. It is something that we did not bring upon ourselves, and yet it hurts us dreadfully.

## Homosexual orientation is a "form" of fallen nature

Secondly, homosexual orientation may be understood as a manifestation and particular form of fallen human nature. Fallen human nature, while forming the ultimate commonality of sinners, is soon differentiated. Like the ripples which big bang theorists would have us believe emerged a few nanoseconds into the history of the universe and led to the ultimate differentiation of matter throughout the galaxies, so there are ripples in the big bang of human sin. One person may possess, or labor under, an orientation or predisposition associated with one family of sins, while another person possesses or labors under an orientation or predisposition associated with a different family of sins. As there is a variety of form with our physical disabilities and disfigurements (there being no such thing as a flawless human body), so with our fallen nature. One person has a fallen nature which predisposes him to violence, another a fallen nature which predisposes him to gluttony, and another a fallen nature which predisposes him to homosexual lust. And these families of sins, though distinguishable, are related because they are all against the life, love, and truth of God.

## Fallen-world phenomenon

Thirdly, homosexual orientation is a fallen-world phenomenon that is a moral evil, and other fallen-world phenomena that are non-moral evils may shed light upon it. Like sickness, death, and drought, homosexual orientation would not have existed were it not for sinful acts (Adam's at the least), even though it is not, in itself, a sinful act. We may say that God is displeased with this orientation (there is a disparity between this orientation and the state of his perfectly fulfilled will for the human race), and that there can be no place for it in the new heavens and new earth. Although it is an *unchosen* evil (like a natural evil such as sickness or like other moral evils such as enslavement to demons), it is not beyond moral evaluation. Hays comments, "it cannot be maintained that a homosexual orientation is morally neutral because it is involuntary."[197] And the Ramsay Colloquium asserts:

> Inclination and temptation are not sinful, although they surely result from humanity's fallen condition. Sin occurs in the joining of the will, freely and knowingly, to an act or way of life that is contrary to God's purpose.[198]

In these ways, predispositions to sin, in order to be fully understood, need to be considered in light of the New Testament's teaching about the subjection of the race to hostile powers as well as in light of its teaching about the individual's personal hostility to God (John 8:34–44; 2 Cor. 4:4; Eph. 2:1–3; Col. 2:13–15). The racist and the demon-possessed may have much in common, as may the homosexual and the enslaved pagan.

## Disorientation further compared with natural evil

Fourthly, further comparison with afflictions (natural rather than moral evils) may illuminate such an inherited (dis)orientation when it is isolated from all of those sinful thoughts, words, and deeds in which it comes to fruition. The mere comparison is, of course, rhetorically and politically highly sensitive. Whereas it may be regarded as appropriate to label as an "affliction" a predisposition or orientation to certain sinful eating behaviors, labeling a predisposition or orientation to certain sinful race-related behaviors as affliction would be regarded as undermining moral responsibility and condoning horrible sin. Likewise, labeling a predisposition or orientation to certain sinful heterosexual sexual behaviors an affliction may be regarded as a joke. But labeling a predisposition or orientation to certain sinful homosexual sexual behaviors an affliction is regarded as offensive, patronizing, and homophobic.

But tricky though the use of such language is, it not only safeguards the important truth that temptation is not sin, it also means that a whole raft of biblical insights, comforts, and warnings may be brought to bear upon the situation of the person possessing such an orientation. To put it most boldly and in the form of a question, is it possible to thank God for natural evil? The answer must surely be "yes." It is not that we thank God for natural evil in and of itself, but we thank him for the righteous, loving, and wise use to which he puts natural evil for his people's good and his own glory. It is possible to give thanks to God for something which, regarded in itself, grieves him; which would not exist without sin and indeed which may be the direct result of the sin of another; which is destined to be entirely absent from the new heavens and the new earth; and which constantly renders me prone to all sorts of temptations while robbing me of much of my power to resist. It is further possible to declare that God has permitted or caused this (natural) evil in order to display his glory in me.

Scripture is full of mysterious and moving reflections upon affliction: the affliction of Job and of the psalmists, the blindness of the man whom Jesus healed in John 9, the death of Lazarus, Paul's thorn in the flesh, and the trials and sufferings of those to whom 1 Peter 1:6–8, James 1:2–4, and the book of Revelation were written. All of these trials result from sin, bring temptation, and grieve a holy and compassionate God. Yet God's use of them may be a matter of thanksgiving and even praise.

The same may be said of God's use of moral evil. The greatest affliction and the greatest moral evil ever – the crucifixion of Jesus Christ – is also the cause for the greatest praise and thanksgiving ever. The crucifixion was the result of the sin of others, would not have taken place without sin, rendered Jesus prone to all sorts of temptations, and robbed him of much of his power to resist. God willed this greatest evil ever, not considered as evil and not in its evil, but rather for the righteous, wise, and loving ends which he would accomplish through it. Hating – and in no way the author of – the sin of the crucifixion, God fully intended the event of the crucifixion for the salvation of the world.

The evils we have considered are either natural evils or moral evils, which someone other than the one suffering perpetrated. These evils demonstrate the way in which a person

may even give thanks to God for his particular disorientations and the peculiar configuration of corruption with
which he wrestles. We are not, of course, thankful to God for
the disorientation regarded in itself as moral evil, but rather
for the righteous, loving, and wise use to which God puts the
particular set of sinful inclinations and sinful failings which
this person has.

If I find myself with an orientation to certain sinful eating
behaviors, sinful race-related behaviors, or sinful sexual
behaviors, then with all the anguish which that brings and
with all my longing to be rid of it, I understand in my saner,
that is to say my godlier, moments that a loving God has a
good and wise purpose in this. There may even be moments
of astonishing grace in which, along with my cry, "Who will
rescue me from this body of death?" (Rom. 7:24), I also find
myself saying words of humble submission and God-ward
confidence such as, "I will boast all the more gladly of my
weaknesses, so that the power of Christ may dwell in me"
(2 Cor. 12:9).

Some evils (natural and moral) will be more painful for
some than for others, and some evils will lead to a greater
temptation to particular sins for some than for others. Some
evils (natural and moral) are removed with time and others
are not. Some diseases (moral or physical) are curable,
others are not. Still others may be incurable and yet it may
be possible to manage the symptoms and to learn strategies
for coping with the associated disabilities. The morally or
naturally afflicted who do learn to boast, with Paul, of
God's sufficient grace will recognize that their afflictions
and corruptions are tools in the Spirit's hands to make them
a particular and unique vessel for a particular and unique
display of the glory of that same grace. Thus they will be,
with Paul, equipped to comfort others with the comfort
with which they themselves have been comforted. As
Alexander Whyte says,

We have no cross to be compared to our corruptions, and when they have chased us close enough and deep enough into the secret place of God, then we will begin to understand and adorn the dangerous doxologies of Augustine and Gregory, Fraser and Fox.[199]

Finally, it is but one step more to regard such evils not only as gift but also as vocation. The Apostle Paul's vocation was not only to "carry," but also to "suffer for the sake of" the Lord's name (Acts 9:15–16). Pushing the limits of language, perhaps we could also say that the different corrupt disorientations with which the people of God wrestle and labor are another manifestation of the "varieties of gifts" that come from the same Spirit.[200] Samuel Rutherford wrote that "the devil is but God's master-fencer, to teach us to handle our weapons."[201] Could it not be the case that God's selection of under-fencers – "demons" of pride, prayerlessness, same-sex lust, and other sinful inclinations – against which his people fight and by which they are trained – is yet another demonstration of his mysterious and gracious ways with sinners?

## Actual sin remains inexcusable

Fifthly, even though Scripture's teachings about affliction may help us to understand homosexual orientation (isolated from those sinful thoughts, words, and acts for which it longs and to which it tends), that still does not excuse its fruition in any transgression of God's law. How newly created Adam moved from unfallen moral mutability to knowing consent to actual sin has taxed some of the greatest theological minds of the church.[202] Likewise, how a sinner moves from "mere" possession of a corrupt nature to knowing consent to actual sin is also a matter of profound complexity. What is clear, however, is that with this move (whether from unfallen moral mutability, in Adam's case, or from "mere" possession of a corrupt nature, in our case) to knowing consent to actual sin comes guilt and responsibility.

Sin remains inexcusable, albeit in varying degrees of heinousness and mercifully forgivable, regardless of the origins or severity of the orientation or predisposition to sin which has led to it. The racist's or the homosexual's orientation may be multifactorially explained, relating to his genetic makeup, early experiences, educational setting, and voluntary or involuntary adoption of societal values. Further, the orientation does render the strength of temptations to particular sins much greater than that experienced by those without such an orientation. Still, sin is inexcusable.

It is also true that a person's fallen nature or disorientation does naturally, immediately, and invariably come to fruition in manifold and deliberate wickednesses in the face of temptation – which is to say, given half an opportunity for it to do so.[203] This is true both of the fallen nature as a whole as well as of those particular forms of fallen nature which we have been considering – those partial disorientations or predispositions to sins that may fall into family groups. Referring to homosexuality, Jones and Yarhouse describe it as follows:

> the state of having homosexual desires is of uncertain moral status but certainly must be viewed as a deviation from the Creator's intent for these individuals and must be seen as representing an occasion for sin (just as does heterosexual lust).[204]

Because all sins deserve punishment, the crucial question is what sinners do with the particular predispositions to sin that their particular fallen nature inflicts upon them. Does the person excuse, cherish, hate, lament, nurture, or restrain the predisposition to sin? The distinction between temptation and sin, and further, between fallen nature in a particular form and its fruition in the historical moment of a human act, holds.

In summary, we can say that human beings in Adam are born with a fallen nature, which consists of a disorientation from God and a predisposition towards evils of various kinds. The particular configuration of that disorientation will vary with each individual but, because sin is one and many, there may be families of disorientations. The variety of disorientations means that one person's ability and desire to resist temptation will be greater in some cases and less in other cases than another person's ability and desire to do so. A person's craving, often deep-seated and unconscious, to succumb to some temptations more than to others is the immediate working of his particular disorientation. None of this is new: it flows simply from a combination of fundamental concepts in dogmatic and moral theology, such as the distinction between natural and moral evil, the distinction between temptation and sin, and the ideas of concupiscence and the "ruling passion."

The fact that I have a deep and strong craving to succumb to a given temptation does not excuse me if I do succumb. The origin of my predisposition to certain sins, the cause of my belonging to a certain family of disorientations, may be multiple. The root cause of fallen nature of any shape is the sin of Adam, which is to say that my orientation to sin comes to me as a result of the sin of others, and yet I am not thereby excused if my orientation to sin comes to fruition in actual sin. I may have suffered from the sins of my parents, my peers, and my teachers in such a way that my resistance to certain temptations is minimal and my craving for certain sinful behaviors is immense. Given what we know of total depravity, the corruption of every dimension of human life by the power of sin, it should not surprise us if at some time it could be demonstrated that orientation to some sins is genetically transmitted. Sin has spoiled our genetic makeup. We should not be surprised if such a predisposition to particular sins is found to be located physiologically in a certain neural morphology. We do not know that this is the case for eating disorders, self-pity, violence, racism, same-sex sexual attraction, or dishonesty. But it would not be surprising, nor would it excuse sin, if it were. While predisposition to sin, orientation to sin, and a fallen nature of a particular shape are not the strict cause of sin, they give no warrant to sin and provide no excuse for sin. According to Jones and Yarborough,

> Even if the homosexual condition of desiring intimacy and sexual union with a person of the same gender is caused in its entirety by causal factors outside the personal control of the person, that does not constitute moral affirmation of acting on those desires. If it did, the pedophile who desires sex with children, the alcoholic who desires the pursuit of drunkenness, and the person with Antisocial Personality Disorder who desires the thrill of victimization and pain infliction would all have an equal case for moral approval of their exploits. At the broadest level all humans are heirs to a predisposition that we have not chosen and that propels us towards self-destruction and evil – our sinful nature. The plight of the homosexual who has desires and passions that he or she did not choose is in fact the common plight of humanity. We all face the same challenge: how are we to live when what we want is out of accord with what God tells us we should want in this life?[205]

## The satanic extreme: calling evil good

Sixthly and finally, at the opposite extreme are those single acts, thoughts, and words that are knowingly given full consent without there even being a particular predisposition toward them. One end of the being-doing spectrum ("being," at the top of Fig. 5.1) is the possession of a disorientation considered apart from its fruition in conscious moral action. At the other end entirely ("doing," at the bottom of Fig. 5.1) lie consciously chosen moral acts of transgressing the law of God with no personal orientation to those particular acts – only the desire to cross God's commands and purposes. Deliberately and with no inherent attraction to the action, a moral agent chooses to call evil good and to engage in lawless activities. "Their foot shall slide in due time."[206]

# Summary and conclusion

Throughout this chapter and Chapter 4, we have seen repeatedly that setting theological propositions about sin alongside the observations of particular sinful actions is illuminating. The biblical doctrine of sin distinguishes between nature and act, between degrees of culpability, and between natural and moral evil. It recognizes that the sin of others may put a person in a position where their temptation to sin is almost irresistible, and it holds those others fully accountable. It accommodates analysis of a sinful practice which is widespread, inherited, physiologically situated, the result of the sin of others, and which flows from deep affliction which God may use to produce sensitive, creative, and morally attractive human beings.

It is impossible to make ultimate sense of sin: the mystery of iniquity is fundamentally irrational. Nevertheless, the theological exploration of radical disorientation in fallen sexuality has this justification: laying biblical truths beside contemporary realities confirms those biblical truths, illumines those contemporary realities, and better equips the servants of God to lay down their lives in confronting sin, comforting the afflicted, and calling sinners to full humanness through the forgiveness and renewal which is found in Jesus Christ and in him alone.

Gerard Manley Hopkins, a man who wrestled long and painfully with the affliction of various disorientations, understood this better than most.[207] Seeing young men leave St. Beuno's College in Wales, where he taught, he wrote his wistful and yet confident sonnet, *The Lantern out of Doors*.

Sometimes a lantern moves along the night,
That interests our eyes. And who goes there?
I think; where from and bound, I wonder, where,
With, all down darkness wide, his wading light?

Men go by me whom either beauty bright
In mould or mind or what not else makes rare:
They rain against our much-thick and marsh air
Rich beams, till death or distance buys them quite.

Death or distance soon consumes them: wind
What most I may eye after, be in at the end
I cannot, and out of sight is out of mind.

Christ minds: Christ's interest, what to avow or amend
There, éyes them, heart wánts, care haúnts, foot fóllows kínd,
Their ránsom, théir rescue, ánd first, fást, last friénd.

For all homosexual sinners, for all sexual sinners, for all sinners of every sort, this is the great need and only hope: Christ, their ransom, their rescue, their first, fast, last friend.

# Appendix

### *Richard Baxter on the move from unfallen moral mutability to actual sin and from "mere" possession of a corrupt nature to actual sin*[208]

The word "flesh" in its primary signification, is taken for that part of the body, as such, without respect to sin; and next for the whole body, as distinct from the soul.

But in respect to sin and duty, it is taken,

Sometimes for the sensitive appetite, not as sinful in itself, but as desiring that which God hath obliged reason to deny.

More frequently, for this sensitive appetite, as inordinate, and so sinful in its own desires.

Most frequently, for both the inordinate sensitive appetite itself, and the rational powers, so far as they are corrupted by it, and sinfully disposed to obey it, or to follow, inordinately, sensual things.

But then the name is primarily taken for the sensual appetite itself, (as diseased,) and but by participation for the rational powers. For the understanding of which, you must consider,

That the appetite itself might innocently (even in innocency) desire a forbidden object; when it was not the appetite that was forbidden, but the desire of the will, or the actual taking it. That a man in a fever doth thirst for more than he may lawfully drink, is not of itself a sin; but to desire it by practical volition, or to drink it is a sin; for it is these that God forbids, and not the thirst, which is not in our power to extinguish. That Adam had an appetite to the forbidden fruit was not his sin; but that his will obeyed his appetite, and his mouth did eat. For the appetite and sensitive nature are of God, and are in nature antecedent to the law. God made us men before he gave us laws; and the law commandeth us not to alter ourselves from what he made us, or anything else which is naturally out of our power. But it is the sin of the will and executive powers, to do that evil, which consisteth in obeying an innocent appetite. The appetite is necessary, and not free; and therefore God doth not direct his commands or prohibitions to it directly, but to the reason and free-will.

But since man's fall, the appetite itself is corrupted and become inordinate, that is, more impetuous, violent, and unruly than it was in the state of innocency, by the unhappy distempers that have befallen the body itself. For we find now by experience, that a man that useth himself to sweet and wholesome temperance, hath no such impetuous strivings of his appetite against his reason (if he be healthful) as those have that are either diseased, or used to obey their appetites. And if use and health make so great alteration, we have cause to think that the depravation of nature by the fall did more.

This inordinate appetite is sin, by participation; so far as the appetite may be said to be free by participation, though not in itself; because it is the appetite of a rational, free agent: for though sin be first in the will in its true form, yet it is not the will only that is the subject of it, (though primarily it be,) but the whole man, so far as his acts are voluntary: for the will hath the command of the other faculties; and they are voluntary acts which the will either commands, or doth not forbid when it can and ought. To lie is a voluntary sin of the man, and the tongue partaketh of the guilt. The will might have kept out that sin, which caused a disorder in the appetite. If a drunkard or a glutton provoke a venereous, inordinate appetite in himself, that lust is his sin, because it is voluntarily provoked.

Yet such additions of inordinacy, as men stir up in any appetite, by their own actual sins and customs, are more aggravated and dangerous to the soul, than that measure of distemper which is merely the fruit of original sin.

This inordinateness of the sensitive appetite, with the mere privation of rectitude in the mind and will, is enough to cause man's actual sin. For if the horses be headstrong, the mere weakness, sleepiness, negligence, or absence of the coachman is enough to concur to the overthrow of the coach: so if the reason and will had no positive inclinations to evil or sensual objects, yet if they have not so much light and love to higher things as will restrain the sensual appetite, it hath positive inclination enough in itself to forbidden things to ruin the soul by actual sin.

Yet, though it be a great controversy among divines, I conceive that in the rational powers themselves, there are positive, habitual, inordinate inclinations to sensual, forbidden things. For as actually it is certain the reason of the proud and covetous do contrive and oft approve the sin, and the will embrace it; so these are done so constantly in a continued stream of action by the whole man, that it seems apparent that the same faculties which run out in such strong and constant action, are themselves the subjects of much of the inclining, positive habits: and if it be so in additional, acquired sin, it is like it was so in original sin.

Though sin be formally subjected first in the will, yet materially it is first in the sensitive appetite (at least this sin of flesh-pleasing or sensuality is). The flesh or sensitive part is the first desirer, though it be sin no further than it is voluntary.

All this set together telleth you further, that the word "flesh" signifieth the sensual inclinations of the whole man; but first and principally, the corrupted sensual appetite; and the mind and will's (whether privative or positive) concurrence, but secondarily, and as falling in with sense.

The appetite, 1. Preventeth reason. 2. And resisteth reason. 3. And at last corrupteth and enticeth reason and will, to be its servants and purveyors.

# 6

# Homosexuality

## Handicap and Gift

### Martin Hallett

The main aim of many Christians who struggle with homosexuality is to become heterosexual. They try every program and ministry available in the hope of changing their sexual orientation. They see this possibility of change as their hope in Christ. I do not believe, however, that is where Jesus wants our hope to be. I wonder if this is one example of how the church has been influenced by our culture?

## Sexuality and the church

It is stating the obvious to say that the media loves discussing, exposing and, they hope, scandalizing the issue of sex and sexuality in the church. Although any type of sex is fair game, homosexuality usually makes the headlines. Even the appointment of bishops makes the news, if the appointment is linked with the homosexual issue. A lot of anger and prejudice surface from all sides of the church debate, from liberals and conservatives alike.

I find it especially frustrating that the "gay" voice that is heard within the church is always a "liberal" one, campaigning for the acceptance of homosexual sex as a legitimate and, some would even argue, biblical alternative to heterosexual marriage. This voice does not, I believe, accurately reflect the situation, experience, and opinions of many Christians within the church, who like myself are aware of homosexual feelings.

There are probably nearly as many Christians with homosexual feelings who do not believe that homosexual sex is right for Christians as there are those who are advocating its acceptance. Apart from one or two people like myself, the majority of these "celibate homosexuals" (for want of a better phrase) are silent. They fear rejection from their (mainly evangelical) friends, but they also feel very uncomfortable with liberal views and believe that "gay Christians" will not understand or accept them either. These people, most but not all of them evangelical Christians, have been contacting True freedom Trust (TfT) since 1977.[209] The majority have been Christians for a long time, and some are church leaders. They are men, women, married, single, old, and young. If only their voice was heard, if only they could be encouraged to speak out, I believe that the church situation, its witness, and ministry, would be vastly different. Perhaps there would even be less of a risk of major splits and divisions in denominations debating the issues of homosexuality.

I wonder if one of our problems as Bible-believing Christians is that we are scared of looking at sexuality, and especially at our own sexuality, in a more positive way. We rightly rejoice in a sexuality expressed within marriage, but we tend to see most other experiences of sexuality simply as "problems" to be "defeated," and "handicaps" to be "healed." We are scared of being perceived as too liberal if we see sexuality too positively. I strongly believe the Bible says that any sex outside male and female marriage is sin and, as David Peterson has clearly explained in Chapters 1 and 2, an example of unholiness.

Sexuality, however, is about much more than sexual behavior, and Scripture continually shows us that even bad things can have value. If that were not the case, most of the stories in Scripture would not be valuable. My aim in what I share, therefore, is to encourage a much more positive attitude to our sexuality – to explore ways in which our sexuality helps us understand ourselves and others; to see how we express it without sex; to find how it draws us closer to God. That last statement may shock many, but I hope that I can justify and explain it.

## My story

Before I became a Christian, about thirty years ago, I was quite happy with my homosexuality and was involved with a circle of good close gay friends. Like many, I considered myself a Christian and used to pray. I didn't really know or understand the Lord Jesus and the truth of the gospel, although I had often heard it in the liturgy at school in England and even went to a Christian youth club. When I became a committed Christian and started reading my Bible, I had to ask questions about my homosexuality. At first I tried to persuade myself that homosexual sex within a monogamous relationship would be acceptable, but what I read in the Bible convinced me otherwise. I realized that what was driving my promiscuous homosexual behavior was basically a desire to be loved in an intimate, special way. I didn't need a degree in psychology to notice that the promiscuity stopped whenever I was involved with a "special person."

At the time of my conversion to Christianity there were two "special persons" in my life – the Lord Jesus and the friend who led me to Christ. This meant, as was my pattern, that the constant search for sex had stopped. The possibility of sex was not an option with my friend, and with all of the exciting new things that were going on in my life, I didn't miss sex at all. I was celibate, without even realizing it. I can remember recognizing my love needs and feeling quite positive and excited at the prospect that now, as a Christian, I could love in a wonderful new way. I didn't have to worry about being loved in return. I no longer had to play the relational games, especially hiding my feelings and "playing hard to get," which I never really mastered anyway.

I became involved in a large evangelical church, where the vicar (Canon Roy Barker) believed in encouraging everyone to express their unique ministry and witness, out of their life experiences. This meant that he saw a lot of potential in me – not despite my homosexuality, but because of it. He encouraged me to share my story with the young people and organized a "consultation" for anyone interested in the issue of homosexuality. He arranged for me to join his lay ministry team – a group that aimed to visit every home in the parish. Looking back, I see that all of this was meant to help me see and share the truth of the gospel. Without realizing it at the time, I was beginning to see my unique value as a follower of Christ, within his body.

At no time was I ever given the impression that my sexual orientation was a problem or handicap that needed to be healed. This may have been because I didn't see it that way and was not struggling at that time with sexual sin. At that time Christians did not discuss homosexuality publicly in the way they do today, therefore most of the people in my church had not been exposed to either gay militants or "anti-gay campaigning" Christians. It was not difficult for me to be open, because I was not struggling with anything sexual of which I was ashamed.

My openness also encouraged others to share their struggles (mainly non-sexual) with me. I did not experience any struggles with my sexuality during my first three years as a

Christian. I had other emotional issues to work through, but even in difficult times I had a positive view of my sexuality. Without realizing it, however, I had become judgemental toward other Christians experiencing frustrations and problems. I would not have knowingly expressed these feelings, or confronted anyone, but they were certainly there.

Then God sent me a "sexual thorn in the flesh" and I became aware of homosexual struggles. It was now a live issue for me again. For the first time in my Christian experience I was struggling with sexual feelings and temptations, just like most other Christians do, regardless of their sexual orientation. I sometimes wonder what my response would have been if this had happened at the beginning of my Christian experience. Perhaps I would have gone back to my old lifestyle. Maybe I would have tried to convince myself that Christianity and homosexual relationships were compatible. But my relationship with Christ and my life within the body of Christ was now so well established that there was, for me, no turning back. There was no alternative but to go on with Christ. I could not entertain any thoughts of forsaking him. So, although I had to work through sexual temptations and sin, I was never tempted to return to my old lifestyle. I wanted to go on with Christ, and I began to see even my struggles as positive. Through them, my sexuality was telling me more about myself, and ultimately more about God's love and forgiveness.

I have met very few Christians with homosexual issues who have a similarly positive experience and attitude towards their sexuality. Although I did not fully appreciate it at the time, my early years as a Christian had encouraged me to see my homosexuality as a vital part of my value and ministry within the body of Christ. This is rare in the evangelical or conservative part of the church today. The majority of Christians who contact TfT find it very difficult to think of their sexuality in any way other than as a problem and a sin with which they continually struggle. Some even question if there are any other sins in their lives. They may recognize that this is far from the case theologically speaking, but because they experience so much anxiety, fear, and guilt linked with their sexual feelings, they find it nearly impossible to see any other sin issues.

I wonder if this is also because we don't emphasize enough the nature of the cross and Christ's redemption in our teaching. We tend to think of the hope we have through Christ in terms of how he changes us and our lives. In other words, we focus on what he *can* do for us, rather than what he *has* done for us. Perhaps we are not able to know how much we are loved by God because we have not been able to believe that we are truly forgiven by him when we sincerely come to his cross for forgiveness. If we were truly experiencing Christ's redemption in our lives, we would long to be made more aware of sins in us which need his forgiveness, thereby enabling us to know his love for us more and more. It seems to me that this is the hope we see in God's word.

I recently looked up every reference to "hope" in the New Testament. None related to what God will do for us in the here and now. All were concerned with final salvation and glorification. Perhaps one of the reasons why we deal so badly with the issue of sexuality in the church is that we expect total transformation in the present. Sex demands so much of our attention because it connects with so many other fundamental issues. It has so much power to influence our thinking. When it therefore causes us so much guilt, we cannot cope with thinking about any other sins that will make us feel even worse about ourselves. Is this why, so often, our attitude as Christians to sexual sin in others actually expresses our own sinfulness in the form of judgementalism, self-righteousness, or even hatred? I guess our human nature and tendency to judgementalism have not changed much since Jesus' time on earth. In some of the (justifiable) campaigning against liberalism in the church, the attitudes expressed and the terminology used seem as sinful as the sexual sin being (rightly) condemned.

# Some experiences of Christians with homosexual issues in the church

When church denominations debate homosexuality, the voice of homosexuals themselves is always one seeking affirmation for homosexual sex, albeit usually within committed relationships. Frequently, the homosexuals speaking out do so with some courage in the face of the opposition they will encounter, especially from evangelicals. If they are ministers and leaders, they also risk losing their ministries because they are speaking against the teaching of their own denominations. Sometimes they come from evangelical backgrounds and have sought to uphold biblical standards while struggling with their sexuality. A change in their theological thinking means, for them, a sense of freedom from the battles and conflicts that had plagued their lives. This sense of freedom gives them even more determination to fight for a change in the thinking of the churches, so that others may be spared, as they see it, from what they define as homophobia.

## Convincing arguments for becoming more liberal?

Many Christians whose theology tends to be very "experiential" become more liberal in their thinking. Someone may have struggled for years with homosexual desires, seeing these desires as a problem without any worth or value. The only way to deal with them is to have them healed and replaced with heterosexual desires. They believe that the only way to deal with these desires is to "heal" them by replacing them with heterosexual desires. The person concerned may seem to accept that this is not going to be simple or easy, but the assumption clearly is that homosexuality is something that a God of miracles never intended and must be able to completely destroy and replace with heterosexuality, which is believed to be "normal."

This form of healing will be a major focus in this person's life, and ultimately marriage will be seen as the proof that this healing has occurred. Sadly, the church often appears to encourage the idea that marriage is the answer to loneliness and sexual frustration, of whatever type. While leaders, and especially married leaders, may not speak of it in these terms, it is an underlying message that comes across. When I ask a single person why he or she would like to be married (and therefore heterosexual), the answer is usually, "I would feel more normal and acceptable." Sometimes I get the same answer if I ask, "Why do you want to be heterosexual?" If I suggest that heterosexual temptations and sin are not better or worse, as far as God is concerned, than homosexual ones, the reply is usually, "But they are normal." In other words, heterosexual sin is more "normal" than homosexual sin.

This somewhat distorted theology of sexuality is buttressed somewhat with the idea that homosexual relationships do not work anyway. People use statistics to prove that many male homosexuals die young and often contract sexually transmitted diseases. They usually do not mention lesbians. The aim, it seems, is to persuade us that God condemns homosexual sex because it is not very good for us and will ultimately, one way or another, cause harm. The statistics are wrongly used to support a theological argument.

With this teaching in mind, some evangelicals meet male and female homosexuals whose relationships seem to be of a very high quality and, rather than being harmful, bring a lot of joy and fulfillment to the people concerned. Christians who see that these relationships can be stable and happy experience cognitive dissonance. If my fellow evangelicals tell me that homosexuality is wrong because homosexual relationships are destructive, and I see that they are not destructive, are homosexual relationships then not wrong at all? I regularly come across this response from Christians working with people with HIV and AIDS in the UK. I hear, "They are such nice people and often, although not always of course, their relationships seem wonderful in terms of love and commitment. It is difficult to see why it should be wrong, when they are just loving one another." A couple of women, possibly in their seventies, were once introduced on a British television talk show. They looked like everyone's favorite grandmothers – they probably did lots of baking and knitted for orphans. The talk show host turned to the evangelicals in the studio audience, where I was sitting, and said, "Elsie and Mabel (not their real names) are lovely, aren't they? They've been in a lesbian partnership for over forty years. How can you tell me this is wicked and sinful?"

Sometimes a Christian struggling with homosexuality is brought up with this idea that all homosexual relationships are emotionally harmful and draw people away from God. Then a Christian relationship in which they are involved starts to express itself homosexually. Much to their surprise, they feel loved and affirmed. This person questions why it should be wrong, because it doesn't appear to have harmed anyone else and it is certainly not hurting him or her. In fact, this person may feel happier and more fulfilled than ever before. In some cases the sex may not have involved any penetration. It is therefore very tempting to convince oneself that it is not wrong and not the kind of homosexual sex the Bible condemns. Christian friends may likewise see what is happening and come to the same conclusion, because the couple feel happier than they have been for years.

In some cases Christians seeing such relationships may be a bit more reluctant and say, "Well at least it's better than the casual encounters they used to feel so desperately guilty about." The homosexual partners pray together and don't feel that God is saying or doing anything to stop the relationship. On the contrary, they actually feel blessed. So their theology changes. They no longer believe Scripture and that God condemns all homosexual relationships. Some would qualify this and say that only penetrative sex is wrong. They may even say that this is the way you should define sex. Heterosexual Christians sometimes use this argument as well. "We haven't had sexual intercourse, just heavy petting." If mutual masturbation and oral sex isn't intercourse, then it doesn't constitute adultery. This is clearly ridiculous. How many married people would believe that their partner was not committing adultery if he or she was masturbating with someone of the opposite sex?

I am trying to illustrate how easy it is for our feelings to persuade us that some "loving" homosexual acts are not displeasing to God. This line of thinking becomes even more convincing when the person expressing it is an evangelical Christian without a homosexual orientation and who is therefore, it may be assumed, unbiased. We must ensure that our theological thinking is based on God's word and an understanding of his holiness, rather than on our feelings or on what appears to be in line with contemporary thinking. In other words, I do not believe God says that homosexual sex is wrong because it will harm us in some way, either physically or emotionally. It is wrong because it is not what he intended human sexual intercourse to be. I think perhaps there was even intended to be an almost sacramental element in sexual intercourse, within the mystery of a "one flesh" marriage relationship, that is, between a man and woman, created in the image of God.

It really saddened me recently when a former T*f*T member, who has become more liberal in his thinking, said, "Now that I believe as a Christian gay relationships are fine, after all these years I accept my sexuality for the first time in my life." It saddened me that he could only accept his sexuality when it involved sex.

## More "open" leaders needed

Many of the Christians who contact T*f*T are actively involved in church life and are often in leadership positions. As ministers and priests and lay leaders within their denominations, they often feel very uncomfortable when their liberal colleagues speak up for homosexual relationships. Although they have to disagree with them, they feel unable to admit their own homosexual feelings. Sometimes unthinking remarks from their fellow evangelicals make them even more fearful of honesty and openness. What a difference it would make to the church debate if these people were to speak out against homosexual relationships and admit that it is a personal issue for them.

A friend of mine in Sweden (Erik) is a Lutheran priest who believes in the traditional biblical teaching on sexuality and has homosexual feelings himself. He determined, from the beginning of his call to the ordained ministry, that he would be open about his sexuality at every stage. Many evangelical newspapers in Sweden have carried his story with his picture and even details of where his church is based. Erik says that this has not caused him any problems with his colleagues or his congregation. He sees his sexuality in a positive way as a part of his ministry as a whole. I hope that, one day, we will see many people with Erik's honesty in our evangelical churches.

The Church of Sweden, like the Anglican church, the Episcopal church, and many other denominations throughout the world, has a strong liberal gay lobby within it. Erik finds, as I do, that those with different beliefs seem unsure how to respond, because we are clearly affirming our sexuality without condoning sex. One or two honest church leaders could start this happening in the UK and we in T*f*T want to encourage and support this. They wouldn't need to necessarily make a big issue of it. They could mention their awareness of personal homosexual struggles and temptations but affirm their conservative biblical beliefs. Clearly such a confession might attract some attention at first, but it may not. Ultimately, as more evangelicals make such a public stand, it will seem less costly and will, I believe, have a tremendous impact for the kingdom of God.

## Liabilities and assets

As I have said, many Christians view their homosexuality as a problem or handicap. They see it only as a liability and never an asset or a part of their value. Some even doubt if they have any other sin problems, which is clearly never true. As Christians, they are constantly fighting against their homosexuality and are unable to think of it or use it in any positive way. Please don't misunderstand. I am not implying that we should stop fighting against sexual sin, but in my experience having such a negative attitude towards our sexuality actually compounds the problems. If I believe that the problems in my life have no value whatsoever, then I will probably find it difficult to believe that I myself have any value.

As we have said above, the main aim of many Christians who struggle with homosexuality is to become heterosexual. They try every program and ministry available in the hope of changing their sexual orientation. They see this possibility of change as their hope in Christ. I do not believe, however, that is where Jesus wants our hope to be. I wonder if this is one example of how the church has been influenced by our culture. There must be a solution for every problem and some way that we can "fix" everything, preferably as quickly as possible. Perhaps as a result, we feel that when we present the gospel we need to make it solve people's problems and difficulties. That is what people want to hear, so we say, "This is what Jesus will do for you," rather than, "This is what Jesus has done for you on the cross and thereby given you forgiveness of sins and eternal life."

I am not trying to say that God doesn't do wonderful things for us in the here and now, but if our hope is based on this are we not more to be pitied? Many people say to me, "What hope can we offer homosexuals? What hope can we offer the Christian struggling with homosexuality?" We cannot say with certainty what God may or may not do in this life, but we can state with absolute certainty the hope that we have in the forgiveness of our sins and God's promise of eternal life.

Christians who share their stories of homosexual struggles are often those who can claim that they have experienced a change in sexual orientation. While this change frequently has actually happened in the person's experience, this person also usually shares his or her need to avoid places of homosexual temptation. The excited listener often does not hear this aspect of the "changed one's" story, however. Such a listener also assumes that what happened in one person's experience will certainly happen in theirs, if he or she follows the same path. Everyone is unique, and that includes our sexuality and all that it involves in terms of its development and expression.

## Marriage and singleness

I know many Christians who never thought heterosexual marriage would be an option for them, because of their homosexuality. Some, however, have continued to work at underlying issues – often linked with their sexuality. They have been able to see themselves more positively and have become more aware of God's love and their own value. This personal sense of value has contributed to their friendships with the same sex becoming more affirming. In other words, they felt more accepted by the same sex. Sometimes friendships with the opposite sex begin to involve some emotional feelings and even occasional sexual ones. Sometimes these couples recognize that they want to spend the rest of their lives together. While they both accept the possibility that homosexual issues may still be around, they do not see this as a threat or as a sign of their lack of desires for each other. These marriages often seem to work well, even if homosexual struggles are still there, because of the confidence in the relationship of mutual love, desire, and commitment.

## Married people with homosexual feelings

I have come across Christians in their sixties and seventies, married with grown children, who are aware of homosexual feelings. These feelings have always been there, to some extent, but the people concerned have often sublimated them with Christian ministry and family commitments. Their partners often seem to be unaware of their spouse's homosexual issues. I think this is often a case of "not wanting to be aware." I would not encourage this route of sublimation and denial for couples considering marriage, but it clearly seems to have worked well for some Christians in the older generation.

In some marriages, the partners' emotional attraction to one another involves a degree of unresolved dependency issues and hurts from the past. For example, Sara was sexually abused by her stepfather and her "natural" mother did not believe her. This experience left her with a need to be in control of her own life and of others involved in it, which was at times inappropriate. She was drawn to men whom she could influence and to some extent "control." Richard has homosexual issues and always felt much closer to his mother, whose strong personality used to influence him, than he did to his father. Richard and Sara got married and, ten years of marriage and three children later, his homosexual struggles surfaced and he met a younger man. He started buying his own clothes and going to gay discos. He said, "I feel for the first time in my life I am doing what I want and not simply living to please others!" Sara felt totally out of control. "I wish he had another woman, rather than a man. At least I could cope with that. I could compete!" Richard and Sara's situation is not an uncommon one. Sometimes the feelings involved are subtler, with just a few of the influences mentioned above. The pattern of two people relating to each other primarily on the basis of their hurts and unmet needs occurs between heterosexuals as well, of course.

Sexual feelings and desires are much more complex and variable than is often appreciated. People often ask, "Will I always have these feelings?" We want to be able to determine exactly what life is going to be like tomorrow. We pay lip service to the fact that it's not that straightforward, but we desperately want it to be so. Many testimonies have been written by Christians who have experienced heterosexual feelings after knowing only homosexual feelings. But we hear far less frequently about Christians experiencing homosexual feelings for the first time, after knowing only heterosexual feelings. I guess we believe that it is not what people want to hear. How tempting it can be to censor our stories from a fear of not being a good witness. Such censorship can sometimes be a subtle form of pride or self-idolatry, which is sin and certainly not biblical.

I have met many happily married women, often involved in pastoral and counseling roles in their church, who find that homosexual feelings have surfaced in an especially close relationship with another woman. They are usually horrified because it is often completely unexpected and had not been part of their experience previously. This seems to be more common with women than with men – probably because women are often more prepared to be vulnerable emotionally. Their sexual feelings may be driven much more powerfully by their emotions than by physical erotic attractions. This is a generalization, of course, and not true for all women or all men. I believe it is very significant that women in this situation often say, albeit reluctantly, "She makes me feel more of a woman than my husband is able to do." This is not usually any reflection on her husband's relationship with her. It has much more to do with the way she feels about herself or the fact that she finds it difficult to love herself.

## Singleness

Those inside and outside the church do not usually see singleness in a positive way. If we are not in a sexual relationship of one sort or another – marriage, in the church's case – we are led to believe that there is something wrong with us. I believe that this comes from a legitimate, God-created desire within us "not to be alone." It is often naively assumed that a stable sexual relationship is the best way of solving sexual frustrations and problems.

The evangelical church is probably influenced by this way of thinking to some extent, but when we talk about sexual relationships we mean marriage. In some cases marriage will bring an end to sexual frustrations, but this is certainly not true in all cases, whether the problems are homosexual or heterosexual. In fact, if there is an addiction issue, sexual activity in marriage may make it even worse. It could be compared, to some extent, with an alcoholic having one glass of wine at a dinner party. It will not quench the desire for more. So a heterosexual man can still be addicted to pornography, even though he is in a good sexual relationship with his wife.

Married people must seek to work through any addiction issues so that they are able to enjoy a fulfilling sexual relationship. The Christian struggling with homosexuality can often harbor the naive assumption that married heterosexuals don't have sexual problems. Some enter marriage, therefore, in the hope that it will mean the end to homosexual struggles. Sadly their Christian friends, especially single men, often encourage this. There aren't enough Christian men available for the single women, and a single man cannot be wasted. This is a bit of an exaggeration, perhaps, but I often hear heterosexuals say of a homosexual man, "What a shame!" "What a waste!" or "I really believe God wants you to be married to her." Single women with homosexual struggles sometimes experience the same pressures, but it is probably less common.

## Nature or nurture?

Christians struggling with more unusual sexual temptations and desires, either homosexually or heterosexually expressed, sometimes contact TfT. I guess because people know that we seek to understand homosexuality, they believe that we may not be shocked by their heterosexual fetishes. Although it is not my area of expertise, it is a fascinating subject.

For example, John says he is sexually excited by wearing an adult nappy. Darren is sexually excited by "soiling" his pants. Such behavior seems to be saying something about their past experiences and relationships including, and probably most importantly, their relationship with themselves. If such a link with the past is fairly obvious in these sexual desires, could that not be the case, to some extent, with all sexual feelings?

I know very little about Freud, but I do believe that there are links between sexual and emotional feelings and our past relationships and self-image. I find that the most helpful way of looking at this process of development is in terms of messages we have received about ourselves and our relationships, and how we have responded. Some of those messages come from circumstances in our lives, perhaps outside anyone's control. Some have come from relationships with our peer group and others. Clearly our parents, or parental role models, are also very significant influences on our emotional and, therefore, on our sexual developmental process. Maybe even our genes affect the way we react to all of these influences in our lives. The messages we have received are not necessarily those intended by their source. For parents, it must often seem like a "no win" situation. You can desire the very best for your children and seek to relate to them in what you think are all the right ways, yet they may still end up with problems and misunderstandings about themselves.

Paul's father, the pastor of a thriving church, has always worked very hard for his family and church members. He had hoped that Paul would do better at college than he did. Paul's mother was more of an extrovert than his dad, and her strong beliefs and the way she expressed them seemed to influence him greatly. As a child, Paul was aware of sometimes feeling jealous of his dad's relationship with Jesus. As a minister's son, he felt a bit left out at school. One of the messages Paul received was that his value was based on what he achieved. This is the last thing either of his parents wanted him to believe.

Paul also wished that he was "one of the lads" or "cool guys" as a teenager. Some children with similar childhood experiences and feelings don't develop homosexual desires, but Paul did. I don't believe he assigns any blame for this, and neither should anyone else. His parents did their best for Paul, but various factors and experiences left Paul with the idea that he is not all that he ought to be. He is usually sexually attracted to athletic young men with a strong personalities

– the kind of person Paul would have liked to be himself. Some people may be homosexually attracted to the person they would like to be now. Sometimes they do have the qualities that they are attracted to in others but find this difficult to believe.

Jane was sexually abused by her stepfather and didn't tell her mother about it until recently. Her stepfather, as is often the case in these situations, always told her that it was their little secret and that it would hurt her mother, who suffered with depression, if she knew. Jane loved her mother, but she was remote from her emotionally – partly because of the abuse situation and partly because of her illness. As an adult, Jane had a few heterosexual relationships, but she experienced homosexual feelings for the first time when she was twenty-eight. She fell in love with a forty-two-year-old mother of four children, who didn't respond sexually to Jane.

Unlike Paul's situation, Jane had a background of traumatic sexual abuse. It clearly affected Jane's relationships with men, but maybe not in the way one might expect. The abuse did not make her not want to have sex with men. She was quite heterosexually promiscuous. However, her relationships tended to be either with abusive men or very passive ones. As a child she felt unprotected by her mother, who was completely unaware of the situation. Because of this, as a child Jane actually withdrew from her relationship with her mother. However, her mother also needed a lot of practical care and support in the home, which Jane helped to provide as a "good little child." The messages Jane received from all of this included, "Your value is dependent on what you do for others," and "You need to be in control of people and your circumstances, otherwise you will be destroyed."

When a mature, motherly, caring woman became significant in Jane's adult life, she seemed to be experiencing what she had never felt as a child. Jane's strong emotional dependency on this woman included some strong erotic feelings also. Again, a combination of circumstances and relationships from Jane's past resulted in her reacting in a way that others may not have. How can her mother be blamed for her poor relationship with Jane, when she was ill and completely ignorant of her deceitful husband's abuse of her beloved daughter? The only one really needing to repent here, of course, is her evil stepfather. While all of the examples I have given are fictitious, except where stated, they are very much like the many situations I have encountered through T*f*T.

Each person's life experience is unique, as are each person's responses. None of us will or can be perfect parents or friends. We can only try our best. None of us have been completely unscarred by our life experiences, which is maybe why none of us can say for certain that we will not have emotional or sexual problems as a result. We should not be intimidated by an unusual sexual feeling or desire because it relates to and "speaks" of issues that most of us have experienced to some extent in our own lives.

## Parents and friends

When we encourage parents not to take unwarranted blame for their son's or daughter's sexuality, this is often difficult for parents to hear and believe. Parents tend to blame themselves in some way or another. They must work through these feelings with God's love and truth, fighting against Satan's lies. This includes experiencing God's forgiveness. Parents often feel that they ought to be able to do something to fix or change the situation, even when they know in reality that this is probably not possible. A parent will often say, after having been told unexpectedly of a son's or daughter's homosexuality, "A part of me thought an aspirin, a hot drink, and a good night's sleep would solve the problem. Then I dismissed it, laughed, and cried!"

A very common reaction to the unexpected revelation of the homosexuality of a spouse, parent, sibling, child, or friend is a tremendous sense of loss. The person I thought I knew seems to have gone. We naturally build up an image of another person with the information we have been given. When this image has developed, perhaps over many years of a relationship, it is shattered by a shocking revelation that takes us completely by surprise. It really hurts us and damages our sense of security. Like any bereavement, it takes time to work through and may even involve some irrational feelings like anger. It is important to recognize this and to give oneself and the loved one time to work this through.

Ongoing communication is one of the main ways to bring healing to the relationship. Sharing feelings and personal information helps to rebuild the identity of the loved one. I believe it is helpful to look at this process as "unwrapping a gift." The gift is one of self-disclosure. You are trusting the other with personal information that can often cost a lot, but it is a wonderful act of love. The process involves helping each other to unwrap this gift by encouraging honesty, love, and acceptance.

We often wonder what we should say to the loved one or friend whose lifestyle conflicts with our belief system. The response I often hear is, "I don't want them to think that, as a Christian, I approve, but I want them to know they are loved." I believe the key is to be honest about your own feelings, doubts, and questions. If you fear how they will react and don't want them to misunderstand, then say that. Because it has probably been difficult for them to anticipate sharing this truth with you, be sensitive to how they may already have decided you will react. They may react defensively in anticipation of your criticism and rejection. You may need to be prepared for misunderstanding as you ask questions in order to better understand them and how they are feeling. I think that this is what Jesus models for us in the Gospels, especially when the woman anoints him and the Pharisees clearly misunderstand the situation. It is important to appreciate the feelings and misconceptions that could be there, even if they are not actually there.

Of course, the other person may not be responding as he or she should and may unreasonably accuse and condemn us. I guess this is often called "transference." The other person transfers the guilt that he or she feels and probably won't admit to you, in order to ease his or her own pain. This can sometimes be discussed, but we will probably be "walking on egg shells" here. At TfT we often meet people who have rejected evangelical Christianity because they feel they cannot live up to what they assume to be its standards. They therefore attack it and its believers. Sometimes there may be some truth in the accusations, but usually they are largely defensive.

I personally believe that, in the homosexual context, this defensiveness has a lot to do with the low self-worth that often drives homosexual feelings. Negative feelings about themselves may drive those struggling with homosexual feelings to be perfectionistic. A sense of failure is ever present and very painful. Sometimes a response to feeling that one has failed as a Christian is to say, "Christianity doesn't work!" Sometimes people may identify one aspect of Christianity as "not working." This in fact has a lot more to do with a deeply painful sense of failure. If I say that something doesn't work, then I can convince myself that I haven't failed and thereby attempt to lessen the pain. When we experience criticism, we often react the same way – by discrediting the person who criticizes us. "What do they know anyway?" Again, sometimes the person can be gently encouraged to see this, but it's not easy. So good, loving, discerning, and honest communication is the key to these relationships – whether with loved ones or in sharing Christ's love. It is far from easy.

# How can we respond corporately and personally?

We must seek to understand and appreciate the dilemma that many Christians face with their sexuality – emotionally, sexually, and socially. How tempting it can be to wander off the "narrow road" of following Christ to the often fulfilling relationships that are available to us if we compromise scriptural truths. We must recognize the challenge we all have to follow Christ, and that it will be costly. We must encourage people to follow Christ because of what he has done for them at the cross, not simply for what he may do for us in this life. "If for this life only we have hoped in Christ, we are of all people most to be pitied" (1 Cor. 15:19).

The person may have a sexual addiction issue, which requires a similar response as with other addictions. Accountability needs to be set up – the person to whom we are accountable is "with us" in our temptations, which can help to lessen the power and secrecy of those temptations. Usually the best person to whom we can give account is the last person with whom we want to have accountability. "Therefore confess your sins to one another, and pray for one another, so that you may be healed" (Jas. 5:16).

We must recognize the low self-worth from which homosexual desires usually originate. We therefore appreciate the way this influences our relationship to God, to others, and to ourselves. We see the potential for low self-esteem affecting our spirituality and Christian discipleship. We replace the lies our feelings have influenced with the truth of our value to God. We repent of believing that God has created us to be unacceptable. We proclaim that truth to others. "I praise you, for I am fearfully and wonderfully made" (Ps. 139:14).

We must present a biblical understanding of hope and healing, so that Christians will not feel disillusioned but will understand the truth of God's love and forgiveness. We must encourage a greater understanding of sexuality, seeing that it is much more than sex and that it connects with many other feelings in our lives. We can learn to understand what our sexuality is saying to us about ourselves, our lifestyles, and relationships. We can then begin to understand what God says to us about it through Scripture as a command for us to be holy as he is holy. "Be holy, for I the LORD your God am holy" (Lev. 19:2 NIV).

We need to appreciate the value of our story and the stories of others, because God is the "potter" or "storyteller." We realize that "valuing" does not necessarily mean condoning or saying that something is good. We accept the mystery of God's ways and accept that we will never fully understand them this side of eternity. "For my thoughts are not your thoughts, neither are your ways my ways," says the LORD. "For as the heavens are higher than the earth, so are my ways higher than your ways and my thoughts than your thoughts" (Isa. 55:8-9).

We need to recognize the ministry that we and others have, not despite our unique stories and situation, but because of them. We are able to experience that ministry as part of the body of Christ. "We know that in all things God works for the good of those who love him, who have been called according to his purpose" (Rom. 8:28, NIV).

We must accept the God-created need for human relationships and develop special relationships of commitment with our brothers and sisters in Christ. Our sense of value to God and the security this brings should empower our relationships of love. We do not, therefore, need to seek this security primarily from our human relationships. We love others more completely when we know that we are loved by God. "'You shall love the Lord your God with all your heart, and with all your soul, and with all your mind.' This is the greatest and first commandment. And a second is like it: 'You shall love your neighbor as yourself'" (Matt. 22:37–39).

# The gift of my sexuality

Working through the choices and processes I have outlined will involve seeking to deal with the issues that surface and that may threaten to hinder the process. Inevitably, many of these issues will have been involved in the development of our sexuality. This may mean that our sexuality changes, but it may not. We will know that we are of value and loved by God and others. We will know that we have a ministry, because of our unique life experience and all that involves. Our sense of identity should therefore be secure, not based simply on our sexuality.

In fact, no two people have exactly the same sexuality – and therefore labels serve only a very limited purpose. I am a "Martinsexual" and you are a ". . . sexual." My life story and experiences, "written" by God, who is sovereign, include my sexuality, which is a gift to the church. It has always been a gift – not just since the ministry of T*f*T began. I am very grateful that I see this experienced nearly every day of my life. I am able to see my struggles and failures, as well as my victories, as being of value to others. This is just as true for the people who contact me for help and support. Listening to their experiences adds to my knowledge and therefore enhances my ministry to others.

This must be true for everyone, whatever our sexuality may be. It can be a gift to others. We may use it to promote more understanding. We may use it to encourage someone else. We may use it simply to love and trust another person with a sexual confession. The list is endless and different for each person and each situation. I am not implying that we should all share our sexual feelings and struggles with everyone. It may not be appropriate or wise – and especially not in the form of a "sound bite," which can easily be misunderstood. But the way that our sexuality can speak to us about ourselves can also help others, explicitly or indirectly.

Perhaps a more positive Christian attitude to sexuality, which honors God's word, would encourage those leaders in the church who have homosexual feelings but who believe homosexual sex is wrong to be more open. As we have seen, their voices are usually not heard in the church debates. Liberals speak on behalf of homosexuals and lesbians in the church but never admit that many of us do not agree with a liberal viewpoint. People like Erik, the Lutheran pastor from Sweden, are not a tiny minority in terms of all homosexuals in the church. There may be nearly as many who disagree with the liberals as those who do. I wish their voices could be heard saying that "We believe our homosexuality is a part of our value and giftedness to the church, but homosexual sex is a sin." What a difference this would make to the life, witness, and future of the body of Christ.

# 7

# Nature or Nurture

## The Causes of Homosexuality[210]

### Peter Saunders

It remains difficult, on scientific grounds, to avoid the conclusion that the uniquely human phenomenon of sexual orientation is a consequence of a multifactorial developmental process in which biological factors play a part, but in which psychosocial factors remain crucially important.[211]

## Introduction

Karoly Maria Benkert coined the term homosexuality in 1869. The prefix "homo" comes from the Greek word meaning "same," the opposite of "hetero," or "other." The *Oxford Dictionary* defines homosexuality as "being sexually attracted only by members of one's own sex," but there is no universally accepted definition among clinicians and behavioral scientists. There is even less agreement as to its cause.

Part of the problem is that not all people are exclusive in their sexual inclinations. There is a spectrum ranging from those who have never had a homosexual thought in their lives, to those who experience nothing else. In the 1940s, Alfred Kinsey conducted a major study[212] into sexuality and classified subjects on a continuum from 0 (exclusively heterosexual) to 6 (exclusively homosexual), with grades of bisexuality (attraction to both sexes) in between.

Another difficulty with definitions is that sexual desire may or may not correlate with sexual behavior. Some people with exclusively same-sex erotic fantasies may never proceed to homosexual activity, and in fact may live in long-term heterosexual relationships. Others with sexual desire only for the opposite sex may, under extreme circumstances (such as in prisons or during wartime), participate in homosexual acts. The term "sexual orientation" is now commonly used to describe the predominant sexual preference.

## Changing perceptions

Medical perceptions of homosexuality have changed. In the nineteenth century it was attributed first to moral degeneracy and later to mental illness. In the early twentieth century it was credited to hormonal imbalance, to psychosocial influences and, more recently, to biological factors. Many now see it simply as a natural variant like handedness or skin color.

As recently as 1967 in the United Kingdom, homosexual behavior between consenting adults in private was a criminal offense at any age. In 1974, the American Psychiatric Association voted to drop homosexuality from its official list of mental disorders (DSM II), and in 1994 the British Medical Association (BMA) Council joined in calls for lowering the age of homosexual consent. This change in perception rests on the presupposition that homosexual orientation is biologically determined and unchangeable, and much of the current literature focuses on the need to help homosexuals embrace their sexuality and cope with discrimination. Some within the American Psychiatric Association are now calling for an official ban on therapy to change the condition (reparative therapy)[213].

Now that homosexuality has attained "non-pathological status," it is increasingly difficult to ask fundamental questions or to carry out research that challenges the prevailing view. As one commentator has put it: "this is an area, *par excellence,* where scientific objectivity has little chance of survival."[214]

The problem is clearly displayed in a 1996 review of the current state of biomedical research on homosexuality. This review concluded that the causes of homosexuality are unknown, that sexual orientation is likely to be influenced by both biological and social features, and that the area could be studied. The review then argued that research into the causes of homosexuality would be unethical and should not therefore occur.[215] Consequently, little work has been carried out recently. A 1997 review of the most likely causes of homosexuality concluded that the scientific study of sexual orientation is, at best, still in its infancy.[216]

## Vested interests

It is difficult not to bring one's own preconceptions to scientific investigation. The temptation (consciously or unconsciously) is to view the facts selectively in order to prove the rightness of one's own prior convictions. Many researchers are quite open about having an agenda other than the mere pursuit of scientific truth. If sexual orientation is not fixed, then according to US law at least, homosexuals may not be protected from "discrimination."[217] Bailey and Pillard, two of the most prolific medical researchers in the field (and leading advocates for the view that homosexuality is inborn) have commented that "a biological explanation [of homosexuality] is good news for homosexuals and their advocates."[218] Another author has suggested that if homosexuality is a purely biological phenomenon, "society would do well to re-examine its expectations of those who cannot conform."[219]

Researchers who have the added motivation of changing public opinion will be guided along certain channels in their work. There are now powerful interests in the scientific community attempting to prove that homosexuality is uniform across time and culture and therefore "natural," that sexual orientation is established early in life, that it cannot be changed even with "treatment," and even that homosexuals are in some way genetically superior and therefore favored in the evolutionary process.[220]

## The influence of media and pressure groups

Journalists can also bring their private social agendas to bear by selective and sensational reporting of research findings. Tenuous conjecture is then interpreted to a gullible public as certain conclusion. Gay rights activists have used sympathetic academics and a supportive press to seek minority status for homosexuals and the abolition of all forms of perceived discrimination. Practicing homosexuals, they argue, should be given equality in the workforce, in social welfare, and in being able to marry and raise (adopted or artificially conceived) children. The strategy, as outlined in books by gay authors such as *The Homosexualisation of America* and *After the Ball*[221] is as follows: "divert attention from what homosexuals do, make homosexuality a topic of everyday conversation, portray homosexuals as normal and wholesome in every other way, and portray those who disapprove of homosexual behavior as motivated by fear, ignorance, and hatred."[222]

It is, of course, quite appropriate for the public to be responsibly informed about scientific discoveries, but twenty-second sound bites cannot do justice to complex controversies, especially when those holding a contrary view are not given the opportunity to respond. "The one who first states a case seems right, until the other comes and cross-examines" (Prov. 18:17).

### Balancing word and world

Of course we have to be careful not to fall into the same trap ourselves, by selectively using scientific findings to bolster our own position. We need to cultivate an open-mindedness which neither gullibly accepts nor quickly rejects new data, but which rather tests the claims of scientists rigorously. The biblical injunction to "inquire and make a thorough investigation" (Deut. 13:14) is surely relevant here.

We can expect that just as the Bible will lead us to question whether we have interpreted the scientific facts correctly, so scientific discoveries may lead us to question whether we have interpreted the Bible correctly. We need to balance revelation and science, the word and the world, in a humble search for the truth – knowing that, properly interpreted, science and the Bible should not contradict each other.

## The limitations of science

When it is next announced by the media (as it inevitably will be) that, for instance, scientists have discovered a "gay gene," or a difference in the brain structure of homosexuals, we should evaluate the evidence for such a claim carefully before jumping to conclusions one way or the other.

First, we need to ask whether the research has been replicated elsewhere. Often other studies will have been published which come to opposite conclusions. If the issue has never been addressed before, we need to wait to see if independent investigators can repeat the study and come to the same conclusions. A classic example of this kind of error was the Kinsey Report.[223] For decades, researchers adopted Kinsey's figure of 10 percent for the incidence of homosexuality in the general population, not realizing that this estimate was based on a poorly designed study of a non-randomly selected sample population, 25 percent of whom were (or had been) prison inmates. The figure stood unchallenged, largely by default, until quashed by contemporary research. The finding in a recent British sex survey,[224] that only one in ninety people had had a homosexual partner in the previous year, is much more in keeping with the figure of 1 to 2 percent now generally quoted. Research published in 2001 indicated that 2.6 percent of both men and women reported homosexual partnerships.[225]

Second, we need to look at the response from the rest of the scientific community. Other researchers may examine the findings of the study in question and not agree that they warrant the claims made. When it was announced in 1993 that homosexual orientation had been mapped to a small section of the X chromosome,[226] the media uncritically propagated the news as fact. However, an editorial reviewing the findings that was published shortly afterwards in the *British Medical Journal*[227] was far more cautious. Not surprisingly, this review was not given the same high profile in the popular press.

Third, we need to ask whether there are confounding variables in the study which could be distorting the results. If subjects for a study are not randomly selected from the general population, or if like is not being compared with like, then the results can be skewed. For example, subjects for a key study claiming to prove that homosexuality has a genetic basis were actively recruited through homophile magazines – hardly an unbiased sampling process.[228]

Fourth, we need to ask whether an apparent link between, say, homosexual orientation and brain structure is a direct effect or not. In other words, does the brain difference cause the sexual orientation, or vice versa? Or, alternatively, is the observed difference a consequence of some third factor such as the disease process AIDS?

Fifth, we must avoid simplistic solutions to complex problems. As science progresses, it becomes increasingly clear that nature is far more complex than we first imagined. With homosexuality, the lack of any real consensus regarding cause should make us suspect that we are not dealing with simple cause and effect.

## Nature or nurture?

Having laid this framework, we now proceed to examine the evidence put forward. What is it that makes one person experience homosexual thoughts while another does not? Is homosexuality something genetic, or is it a result of upbringing? Is it biological or psychosocial? Or, to use biblical terminology, are people "born that way" or "made that way by men"(Matt. 19:12)? Furthermore, if nature or nurture (or both) are involved, then what part does personal choice play in a person adopting a homosexual lifestyle?

Opinions on these questions differ widely among leading researchers. Some, like Boston psychiatrist Richard Pillard, conclude that "homosexual, bisexual and heterosexual orientations are an example of the biologic diversity of human beings, a diversity with a genetic basis."[229] Others, like Van Wyk and Geist, contend that "biologic factors exert at most a predisposing rather than a determining influence."[230] Still others hold the middle ground. Let us review the evidence.

### Nature arguments

Those who advocate a biological cause have argued that homosexuals possess different hormonal mechanisms, brain structure, or genotype. Such biological explanations may not be unrelated, as genes lay the blueprint for hormones, which in turn influence body structure. We will look at each in turn.

## 1. Hormonal mechanisms

Hormones are chemical substances produced in the body, which have specific regulatory effects on particular body cells or organs. Male sex hormones, or androgens, are produced by the testis and are responsible for the development of secondary sex characteristics like chest and pubic hair and a deepened voice. Female sex hormones, or estrogens, are produced by the ovary and bring about pubic hair growth and breast development. The release of these sex hormones, and indeed the development of the gonads (testis and ovary) themselves, is in turn regulated by other hormones called gonadotrophins (LH and FSH), produced in the pituitary gland at the base of the brain. These are in turn regulated by a third group of hormones (releasing factors) produced just above the pituitary in a part of the brain called the hypothalamus. A delicate balance is maintained.

At one stage it was thought that homosexuals were hormonally different (e.g., in their circulating levels of reproductive hormones), but this idea was abandoned when sensitive hormone assays became available and accurate measurements could be made.[231] However, the possibility remains that hormones might play a part in the *prenatal development* of the brain, and hence in sexual orientation and behavior.

Female rats exposed to androgens in early development exhibit "mounting," a typically male sexual response.[232] By contrast, neonatally castrated male rats exhibit "lordosis," a sexually receptive back-slouching position characteristic of females.[233] Is the rat brain being hormonally programmed in some way during fetal development? Could the same sort of thing be occurring in humans who later show homosexual tendencies?

There are limits in extrapolating these rodent studies to human beings. First, sexual behaviors in rats are under rigid endocrine (hormonal) control. By contrast, in humans sex is not a reflex but a complex and conscious behavior. There is no human equivalent for stereotyped "lordosis" or "mounting." Second, human homosexuals engage in both receptive and penetrative intercourse, whereas in this model "mounting" and "lordosis" were gender-specific. Third, the prenatal hormone theory fails to explain the complexity and variability of the human sexual response with changes of erotic fantasies, modes of sexual expression, and indeed even sexual orientation over time.

If the prenatal hormone hypothesis were correct, we would expect to find a higher incidence of abnormal gonadal structure or function in homosexuals. We do not. We would also expect to find a higher proportion of homosexuals among patients with disorders involving androgen excess or deficiency. Again, extensive reviews of the literature suggest that this is not the case.[234] For example, there is no evidence that children resulting from hormonally treated pregnancies develop homosexual tendencies.[235]

Some very rare medical conditions, in which the affected person's sexual status is ambiguous, have, however, been put forward as providing evidence for a hormonal cause of homosexual orientation. One example is testicular feminization. Affected individuals are genetically male (i.e., they have XY chromosomes) and have testes which are normal but remain in the abdomen. They also have female external genitalia that appear normal. Often these individuals do not come to medical attention until after puberty, when they present with amenorrhea (a failure to menstruate) and infertility. On psychosexual testing they are indistinguishable from heterosexual genetic females in terms of sexual arousal and erotic imagery.[236] However, because they are raised as females (because they look like females), this does not prove that sexual preference is hormonally programmed, rather than environmentally conditioned.

Congenital adrenal hyperplasia is a condition in which genetic females are exposed to excessive levels of androgens produced by the adrenal gland, resulting in masculinized (part-male, part-female) genitalia. The vast majority of women with congenital adrenal hyperplasia develop hetero-sexual interests, and there is no consistent evidence for an increased incidence of lesbianism with this condition. Even if this were shown to be the case, it would be almost impossible to demonstrate that this was due to a hormonal effect on the brain rather than the psychological effect of having mas-culinized genitalia.

Of course, it needs to be stressed that the vast majority (more than 99 percent) of homosexual people have no meas-urable hormonal abnormality. The case for a hormonal cause of homosexuality remains as yet unproven.

## 2. Brain structure

Could homosexuality be the result of differences in the struc-ture of the brain? Again, studies in rodents have aroused sus-picions. The hypothalamus, situated at the base of the brain, is an important hormone control center. Within its substance lie "nuclei," tiny bundles of nerve cells, each no bigger than the head of a pin. Because of their minute size they can only be properly examined in an autopsy. In rats one of these nuclei (SDN-POA) is sexually dimorphic – that is, it is a dif-ferent size in males and females. This finding has fueled speculation that similar differences may exist in humans – not only between sexes, but also between homosexual and heterosexual people. Much current research involves examin-ing microscopic portions of postmortem brain tissue, in attempts to prove that these variations exist.

In 1984, two scientists named Swaab and Fliers claimed to have found a hypothalamic nucleus that was larger in men

than in women.[237] Later, however, they were unable to establish a link between its size and sexual orientation.[238] In 1991,
a neurobiologist named LeVay dissected the brains of thirty-
five males and reported that the size of another hypothalamic nucleus (INAH3) in the homosexual men was smaller
than its counterpart in heterosexual men and the same size as
that of the women.[239] The study was highly publicized, but
again there were reasons to be cautious. Firstly, the numbers
involved were small. Secondly, most of the homosexual men
with abnormal hypothalamuses had died of AIDS. Thirdly, it
was not apparent how the anatomical area involved could
have had a bearing on sexual behavior. Fourthly, even if it
could have had such a bearing, it would remain to be proven
that the structural change was the cause, rather than the
result, of the altered sexual orientation. Finally, other
researchers have pointed to technical flaws in LeVay's
research methodology[240]. A more recent study has corrobo-
rated LeVay's reports of sexual dimorphism of INAH3 but
provides no support for previous reports of sexual variation
in other hypothalamic nuclei.[241]

In addition to the hypothalamus, the commissures (bundles of nerve fibers joining the two sides of the human
brain) have been extensively examined. Allen and Gorski,
again in a well-publicized study, reported in 1992 that the
anterior commissure was smaller in heterosexual men than
in homosexual men and heterosexual women.[242] However,
there was considerable overlap between the three groups,
and again the majority of homosexual subjects had AIDS.
A review of the data in 2002 found that the results of different studies conflicted, and there was no evidence of this
variation.[243]

There have also been claims that the corpus callosum (a
much larger commissure) may be female-typical in homosexual men, but the twenty-three studies reported thus far have
yielded conflicting results.[244]

In summary, we have currently uncorroborated reports that three different brain structures may possibly show structural variation with sexual orientation. However, in each study the sample size was small, the possible relation between the structure and sexual preference has not been established, and the confounding effect of AIDS has not been adequately addressed.

## 3. Genetic studies

In the human body there are a hundred trillion cells, each possessing a nucleus containing more information than an average laptop computer. This information is written on forty-six chromosomes, arranged in twenty-three pairs, with each pair consisting of one chromosome from each parent. The chromosomes are constructed from coils of a ladder-shaped molecule called DNA, which makes up our genes. The genetic language has an alphabet of four letters (bases), and if we were to take the entire amount of information in any one cell nucleus and print it out a thousand letters to a page, it would fill three thousand books of a thousand pages each. The letters are grouped together into three-letter words (codons), strung together into sentences (genes). Each of the thirty thousand genes in the body carries the instructions for the production of a specific protein. Proteins perform a vast variety of actions – from determining the detailed structure of our organs, to transporting chemical substances from one part of the body to another, to controlling the thousands of chemical reactions that are occurring in our different cells. In so doing, genes govern everything from handedness to eye color, from appearance to temperament.

There are about six thousand known genetic diseases (disorders resulting from spelling mistakes in the genetic language which can be passed on from parents to children), and twenty-one thousand children in the UK are born with one of these diseases each year. These conditions vary widely, however, in their severity, frequency, mode of inheritance, and expression. Some are lethal (such as those causing many miscarriages), while others may produce no discernible effects at all. Some (like Down's syndrome) are common, while others are extremely rare. Some (like Huntington's disease), if passed from a parent will be expressed in the next generation, while others (like cystic fibrosis) may skip generations completely or simply create a predisposition for the disorder rather than guarantee its occurrence.

Could homosexual orientation have a genetic component? Could it even be entirely genetically programmed? The possibility of a genetic basis for homosexuality has been recognized ever since Kallman evaluated the twin siblings of homosexuals and found that 100 percent of identical twins, but only 12 percent of non-identical (fraternal) twins, were also gay.[245] While he used a biased sample (most were mentally ill and institutionalized men), and his results have never been reproduced, there have been further studies attempting to show that homosexuality runs in families. The most famous of these are two studies by Bailey. The first showed that 52 percent of the identical twins of gay men were also gay, while only 22 percent of non-identical twins were.[246] The second study gave corresponding figures of 48 percent and 16 percent for the twin sisters of gay women.[247]

There are reasons to be cautious about assuming that these observed effects were due to genes rather than upbringing. First, identical twins are more likely to be treated similarly by parents and others, especially if they have similar temperaments. Even within the same family, children are raised in quite different ways. The fact that non-twin brothers are less likely to share a homosexual orientation than non-identical twin brothers suggests that environment plays a large part – because non-identical twins and non-twin siblings share the same proportion of genetic material. Second, neither study drew subjects randomly but recruited them through homosexual-oriented periodicals. This must, at the very least, introduce the possibility that twins wanting to establish that homosexual orientation is genetic may have been more ready to apply. Was the sampling really unbiased? Third, there has so far been only one small and inconclusive study comparing the sexual orientation of twins who have been reared apart since birth. This variable is, in fact, the best way of ensuring that environmental factors do not confuse the picture.[248] Fourth, even if homosexual orientation is influenced by genetic factors, the presence of a "gay gene" is not necessarily proven. We may simply be talking about a character trait, which makes a child more likely to be treated in a way that might lead to the development of a homosexual orientation. Fifth, the authors' interpretation of their data has been cast into serious doubt by statistical reanalysis which found no difference between the groups.[249] Finally, even if we accept Bailey's results, there is still a large proportion of identical twins (about 50 percent) who develop different sexual orientations, despite allegedly sharing the same prenatal and family environment.

With the rapid advances in our ability to unravel the genetic code, researchers are now trying to discover where on the 46 chromosomes each of the thirty thousand known human genes is located. This international collaborative effort, known as the human genome project, is now well under way and, understandably, there are attempts to locate a gene for homosexual orientation.

In 1993 Hamer, a geneticist working in the field, claimed to have done just that in a paper published in the journal *Science.* He reported that thirty-three of forty homosexual non-twin brothers had homosexual relatives on their mothers' sides with similar DNA markers in a region of the female X chromosome known as Xq28.[250] There was considerable media interest in what came to be known as the "gay gene" but also, as mentioned, less enthusiasm in the medical press.[251] An article in *Nature* commented, "Were virtually any other trait involved, the paper would have received little public notice until the results had been independently replicated."[252] The study sample was small, other researchers have not yet confirmed the results, and there is not as yet any indication of how frequent the Xq28 sequence is in the general population. One researcher who reanalyzed Hamer's data stated, "Using the more appropriate (statistical) test I compared several pairs of relatives . . . there is no evidence for a maternal effect . . . Until these results are replicated . . . they should be viewed with extreme scepticism."[253] Criticism of this study has continued, and few people now give much weight to its evidence.[254]

In fact, no "gay gene" as such has so far been located, let alone had its component DNA sequenced. Even if such a gene is discovered, this may simply carry the instructions for a character trait rather than homosexual orientation as such. Furthermore, even if a genetic link is established for a small proportion of individuals in one section of the gay community, it does not follow that it underlies or explains all homosexuality in all individuals. We know, for example, that a small proportion of breast cancer, but by no means all, is linked to one particular predisposing gene.

As we have seen, interest has focused on finding a "gay gene" in other species. Biologists Ward Odenwald and Shang-Ding Zhang at the National Institutes of Health in Bethesda, Maryland, created a storm of media publicity with their claim to have transplanted a gene into fruit flies which produced homosexual behavior.[255] As it transpired these flies were bisexual rather than homosexual, and no lesbian flies were produced. The complexity of the human sexual response, in comparison with the far simpler reflexes in invertebrates, should lead us to beware of hasty conclusions.

Overall, there is some evidence in small studies that genes may have some bearing on the later emergence of a homosexual orientation. However, many questions remain. If homosexual preference (as opposed to homosexual behavior) were truly genetic, why is it not observed in species other than human beings? Why do a large proportion of identical twins vary in their sexual orientation? Why does sexual preference change over time, or with therapy? Masters and Johnson, in a five-year follow-up of sixty-seven exclusively homosexual men and women, reported that 65 percent achieved successful changes in their sexual orientation after behavior therapy.[256] This has been confirmed by more recent research.[257] Clearly we are not dealing with a simple causal link.

Genetic factors may play a part in the development of homosexual orientation, but they are not the full story. Terry McGuire, Associate Professor of Biological Sciences at Rutgers University, New Jersey, urges us to be circumspect about alleged research findings:

> Any genetic study must use (1) valid and precise measures of individual differences, (2) appropriate methods to ascertain biological relationships, (3) research subjects who have been randomly recruited, (4) appropriate sample sizes and (5) appropriate genetic models to interpret the data . . . To date, all studies of the genetic basis of sexual orientation of men and women have failed to meet one or more of the above criteria.[258]

A subsequent study of approximately three thousand randomly picked people estimated the hereditability of male homosexuality in a range of 0.28–0.65.[259]

While we may not ever find a "gay gene," there is increasing evidence to suggest that personality variants (in particular novelty seeking, harm avoidance, and reward dependence) may well be inherited.[260] These could theoretically predispose a person to the development of a homosexual orientation given the right (or wrong) environment. This leads us to evaluate the role of nurture.

## Nurture arguments

The pure biological view is that homosexual orientation is programmed in the genes, fashioned by hormones, and displayed in brain structure. The pure psychosocial view is that the environment writes upon the developing child, in the same way that someone might draw lines on a blank sheet of paper. Both embrace a type of determinism. In the first, the individual is the product of the interactions of chemical reactions. In the second, he or she is programmed by social forces.

As with the biological arguments, we will consider nurture arguments under several headings, although it should be obvious that they interrelate. Let us consider, then, the cultural environment, the family environment, the peer group environment, and the moral environment.

### 1. The cultural environment
The cultural view is that sexual conduct is determined by the society in which one grows up. In other words, we learn sexuality in much the same way that we learn cultural customs. Whereas biological sex is set at birth, gender-specific behavior develops in a cultural context. The interplay of tradition, religious belief, and political factors lays a framework for acceptable behaviors that become increasingly ingrained until they eventually feel natural.

The evidence for this view is the diversity of sexual behavior across cultures and across history. There are cultures in which homosexual behavior is so uncommon that there is no word for it in the language.[261] Similarly, homosexuality in the form of long-term relationships between consenting adults did not seem to exist in Western culture before the nineteenth century – at least not in any significant frequency.

## 2. The family environment

Most nurture theories focus on the pattern of the parent-child relationship. Male homosexuals are more likely to emerge from families where the father is disinterested, remote, weak, or overly hostile and the mother is the dominant disciplinarian and warmest supporter.[262] In the same way, lesbians may result from families where there is a breakdown of the mother-daughter relationship.

This view has been popularized by Elisabeth Moberley, who has come to the conclusion that homosexual orientation is the result of unmet same-sex love needs in childhood.[263] Martin Hallett, director and counselor at True freedom Trust,[264] a Christian ministry to Christians struggling with homosexuality, has found that the majority of male homosexuals counseled identify very much with this lack of intimate bonding with the father or any other male role model.[265] As a result, the heterosexual identity is not established, and the unaffirmed child suffers later, as an adult, from a lack of confidence and fear of failure in heterosexual contacts. He tries to meet those unmet same-sex needs through sexual relationships. When these fail to satisfy, the result may be an even more compulsive and promiscuous lifestyle.

Sara Lawton,[266] a Christian counselor specializing in lesbianism and sex abuse, similarly sees the root of female homosexuality as an unmet need for mother love, which becomes sexualized in the adult. This can be compounded by repressed trauma (e.g., the mother wanted to abort her), adoption, prolonged separation through illness, or sexual abuse.

The parent-child relationship can also be disturbed through death or divorce. Saghir and Robins found that 18 percent of homosexual men and 35 percent of lesbians had lost their father by death or divorce by the age of ten. The figures for male and female heterosexuals were 9 percent and 4 percent, respectively.[267] The vast majority (up to 70 percent) of homosexual adults describe themselves as having been "sissies" or "tomboys" as children.[268] This is despite the fact that most adult homosexuals fit neither the effeminate male nor masculine female stereotype. While a higher percentage of homosexuals than heterosexuals exhibit some degree of gender nonconformity, we cannot generalize to all cases.

Heterosexuals can come from situations of poor same-sex bonding, whereas homosexuals can come from families where the parent-child relationships were good.[269] However, amidst the enthusiasm to find a biological cause, the extensive experience of counselors and the memories of homosexuals themselves need to be taken into account. Thomas Schmidt, in an excellent, wide-ranging review of the literature, has commented:

> since developmental theory is now out of fashion, homosexuals are either not asked about or no longer "remember" childhood problems. It is certainly suspicious that, to my knowledge, not a single study of early childhood among homosexuals has been conducted since the early 1980s.[270]

## 3. The peer group environment

The formation of a homosexual identity takes time. Before adolescence, most people consider themselves heterosexual, and for the majority these thoughts are reinforced by the peer group. However, for the child who doesn't "fit in" – the masculine female or the non-masculine male – identification with the opposite sex peer group may prove easier, especially if there is experience of rejection by same-sex peers. The male child in this situation may be socialized as a girl, and vice versa. This can lead to gender confusion in adolescence and later identification with others of the same sex who are suffering from the same feelings of isolation. In this context, the acceptance of the homosexual label can bring security, self-understanding, and acceptance at a level which that individual has never before experienced.

Identification with the gay culture, or "coming out," has many rewards in terms of escaping from conflict, reducing the pain of rejection, and providing human contact. In other words, just as peer pressure enhances a sense of sexual identity in those who eventually become heterosexual, so peer pressure can similarly reinforce homosexual feelings and behavior. A network of supportive friends and perhaps a long-term homosexual relationship can be powerful forces driving people into, and keeping them within, the gay community.

Whether heterosexuals can be recruited into homosexuality is a complex issue, but a disproportionate number of male homosexuals were sexually molested as children. Education promoting the idea that homosexuality is just a genetically programmed normal variant will certainly lessen any stigma and make it easier for those with confused gender identity to enter the gay community.

## 4. The moral environment

In all societies, children grow up with a set of instilled values giving them a sense of right and wrong. The parental environment will, to a large extent, shape the conscience. Children who are seldom punished will quickly cease to feel guilt when they cross boundaries. On the other hand, if standards are arbitrarily or unfairly imposed, or if the parents are not themselves good role models, children may rebel against their consciences.

Personal conscience can thus be underdeveloped through upbringing, or blunted through disuse. These effects will be intensified if the public conscience itself is changing, as it certainly is with regard to homosexuality. When homosexuality was regarded as degeneracy, there were powerful social pressures preventing its expression. Now that one can incur the wrath of the politically correct for suggesting that homosexuality is anything other than a natural variant, the tables have turned.

My own opinion concurs with that of Bancroft:

It remains difficult, on scientific grounds, to avoid the conclusion that the uniquely human phenomenon of sexual orientation is a consequence of a multifactorial developmental
process in which biological factors play a part, but in which
psychosocial factors remain crucially important.[271]

# The role of personal choice

Some argue with advocates of a strong nature or nurture
model by claiming that sexual orientation is a myth, and that
homosexuality is a matter of simple choice. This is under-
standable. All of us have a sense that, at least in some small
way, we are the masters of our own destinies. We are not
solely genetic machines any more than we are blank slates on
which experience writes. While most authors recognize the
possible importance of both nature and nurture, often too
little attention has been given to the ways in which these factors interact, or to the role of personal choice.

At some point, every practicing homosexual makes a choice
to indulge in homosexual fantasy, to identify with the gay
community, or to have homosexual sex. And regardless of the
strength and power of the temptations encouraging that
choice, regardless of the biological and psychosocial forces
operating in any individual, from a biblical point of view that
choice is always wrong. However, we must not make the mistake of ignoring the role of nature and nurture in making
those of homosexual orientation what they are. Having a
homosexual orientation is not often a matter of choice.

# An interactive model

While there will always be those who support one model of
causation – be it nature, nurture, or choice – above all others,

the majority of scholars concede that many factors are involved. Heredity and environment are both important, and personal choice is clearly involved too. How these elements interact in any one individual may differ, and this explains why one or more of the biological or psychosocial ingredients may be lacking in any one case.

For example, a boy with a biological predisposition to "girlish" behavior is born into a dysfunctional family where the father is remote and the mother is smothering. He grows up with little moral training in a society where homosexuality is viewed as a normal variant. He experiments with homosexual behavior in adolescence and finds companionship and identity through a long-term homosexual relationship at his university, before entering the gay subculture in a large city.[272] The process may be interrupted or diverted at any point – if the biological disposition is not there, if the family dynamics or society's attitudes are different, or if a conscious choice is made not to proceed. But the process is complex and multifactorial, different for each individual.

This should leave us with a humble and open attitude, willing to learn more from scientific research and the testimony of skilled counselors and gay people, so that we can come to understand and respond appropriately to the factors involved in any individual case.

## What is natural?

Explaining *how* a homosexual orientation may develop, and understanding *why* some individuals are more susceptible than others, does not start to answer the question of how people should behave. There is often an unstated assumption that strong feelings should determine behavior, whereas this is not in fact accepted in almost any other area of life. We do not believe, for example, that a strong desire to smoke or to drink should be rewarded with the provision of cigarettes or alcohol. Nor do we accept that lust legitimizes adultery or that envy sanctions stealing or greed.

Many of the desires we have, if acted upon, lead to damaging not only other human beings but ourselves as well. As the Bible succinctly puts it: "There is a way that seems right to a person, but its end is the way to death" (Prov. 14:12), or "the heart is deceitful above all things and beyond cure" (Jer. 17:9, NIV). God calls us to resist evil desires – not to act on them, but rather to obey him with the strength his Spirit gives.

The gay rights lobby presupposes that what comes naturally is good. By contrast, the biblical worldview is that the whole world, and human beings themselves, are polluted by sin which has affected our bodies (and this must surely include our genes), our minds, our wills, and our feelings. Consequently, our biology, our thoughts, our choices, and our desires are not what they were intended to be. In the biblical scheme, "natural" (as in Rom. 1:27) means not "what comes naturally" but rather "what God intended (and intends) us to be."

## Summary

This complex subject has been helpfully reviewed recently by a variety of Christian authors,[273] and this chapter is itself a revision of previously published reviews of my own.[274] But, in fact, not much has changed in the research area in the last five years.

While Christians will see both homosexual orientation and behavior as evidence that we live in a fallen world, we must not retreat into a simplistic analysis that sees homosexual behavior simply as arbitrary personal choice. The exact means by which sin exerts its effects on societies and individuals is only in part discernible to us as sinful human beings. It should come as no surprise to discover that sin should affect even our genetic code, hormonal functions, and body structures. The aging process itself, for example, is a consequence of sin and yet mediated by these same factors. Why not then a predisposition to homosexual orientation? In the same way, we should not be surprised that our upbringing may have profound effects on our temperaments and personalities.

This is not to deny that all of us, homosexual or heterosexual, are sinners by choice. But we are also sinners by nature, both by virtue of living in a fallen world and by being sinned against by others.

Regardless of what may come to be known in the future about the relative contribution of nature, nurture, and personal choice to the development of homosexuality, its complete healing will only be found through repentance, faith, forgiveness, regeneration, and ultimately resurrection of the body in a new heaven and a new earth.

# Postscript

Trouble and distress have come upon me, but your commands are my delight. Your statutes are for ever right; give me understanding that I may live (Ps. 119:143-4 NIV).

These words describes the struggle, but also the confidence of a child of God. The pressure may be external - to conform to the world or to be persecuted. It may be internal - to give way to temptation or to despair. Whatever its source, the pressure seems ongoing and stressful. Believers today can identify with the Psalmist in a whole range of everyday situations.

Sexual temptation is one expression of this struggle. Those who have homosexual desires may consider themselves a special case, but others too experience powerful sexual temptation, either as single or as married people. The complexity of our personalities makes each situation different, but the struggle to be faithful to God is shared by all true believers. How much better it would be if we could all honestly admit this and support one another more effectively! Perhaps the charge of homophobia would be less common if heterosexuals more readily acknowledged the battles they experience and sometimes lose. Christian fellowship would become more an experience of confession, forgiveness and healing (cf. Jam. 5:16).

Remarkably, in the midst of his struggle, the Psalmist articulates his continuing delight in God's commands. God's revelation itself can be the source of trouble and anguish, because it sets the believer on a collision course with other values and demands, both personal and societal. God's children only delight in his commands when they recognise that they express his will for those he loves and that all his commands are perfect, bringing blessing to those who keep them. The faithful delight to do his will because his own Spirit is at work within them.

Although the Psalmist says "Your statutes are for ever right", some participants in the current debate would question whether this is so. Do the Old Testament regulations about sexual behaviour have any ongoing relevance in the Christian era? Does even the teaching of the New Testament in this connection have any ongoing application in the light of contemporary scientific arguments about the genesis of homosexuality?

This book has argued that there is a consistency of teaching about marriage and sexuality in the different forms of biblical literature, across a range of contexts, and with different sanctions. Holiness is the theological framework in which much of this material is presented. "You shall be holy, for I am holy" is the continuing challenge for God's people in every age and it is God himself as the Holy One who determines what practical holiness will mean. Only those who recognise the consistency of teaching about marriage and sexuality in Scripture will be able to endorse the confession "Your statutes are for ever right".

However, even such confidence should lead us to pray "give me understanding that I may live". It may be understanding about why God's decrees are expressed in the way they are and why they are important for us to obey. We may need understanding about how we can keep his commands, finding the strength and support to be faithful. We may need understanding about what in our past or present experience hinders us from pleasing him and living in his way.

The Bible encourages us to be honest about our struggle with sin and not to mask it. We are to be repentant before God and patient with each other. We are to welcome and to love all who seek God's mercy in Christ and "grace to help in time of need" (Heb. 4:16). But to function effectively as the holy people of God we are not at liberty to alter his demands or to ignore what contradicts his will. We can only uphold one another in the struggle against sin when we identify it for what it really is and care about its destructive effect in ourselves and others. Then, the delight, the understanding and the life of which the Psalmist spoke will be truly ours.

# Bibliography

The books marked with an asterisk are especially recommended for those wishing to gain a broad and representative perspective on this subject.

Altman, D. *The Homosexualisation of America* (Boston: Beacon Press, 1982).

Atkinson, D. J., and D. H. Field, eds. *New Dictionary of Christian Ethics and Pastoral Theology*. Leicester: IVP, 1995.

Allen, L., and R. Gorski. "Sexual Orientation and the Size of the Anterior Commissure in the Human Brain." *Proceedings of the National Academy of Sciences, USA* 891 (1992): 7199–7202.

Bailey, D. S. *Homosexuality and the Western Christian Tradition*. London, Longmans, Green, 1955.

—. *The Man-Woman Relation in Christian Thought*. London: Longmans, Green, 1959.

Bailey, J., et al. "Heritable Factors Influence Sexual Orientation in Women." *Archives of General Psychiatry* 50 (1993): 217–23.

Bailey, J., and R. Pillard. "A Genetic Study of Male Sexual Orientation." *Archives of General Psychiatry* 48 (1991): 1089–96.

Bailey, K. "Paul's Theological Foundation for Human Sexuality: 1 Cor. 6:12–20 in the Light of Rhetorical Criticism." *Near East School of Theology Theological Review* 3 (1980): 27–41.

Bancroft, J. "Homosexual Orientation: The Search for a Biological Basis." *British Journal of Psychiatry* 164 (1994): 437–40.

Banks, R. J. *Jesus and the Law in the Synoptic Tradition.* Society for New Testament Studies Monograph Series 28. Cambridge: Cambridge University Press, 1975.

Baron, M. "Genetic Linkage and Male Homosexual Orientation." *British Medical Journal* 307 (1993): 337–38.

Barrett, C. K. *A Commentary on the First Epistle to the Corinthians.* 2nd ed. London: A. & C. Black, 1971.

Baxter, R. *The Practical Works of Richard Baxter.* Morgan, PA: Soli Deo Gloria, 2000.

Bell, A., et al. *Sexual Preference: Its Development in Men and Women.* Bloomington, IN: Indiana University Press, 1981.

Berkouwer, G. C. *Faith and Sanctification.* Grand Rapids, MI: Eerdmans, 1952.

Best, E. *A Commentary on the First and Second Epistles to the Thessalonians.* Black's New Testament Commentaries. London: A. & C. Black, 1977.

Bledsoe, R. "Envy, Scapegoating and Neurosis." Series of addresses at the Biblical Horizons Conference, Niceville, FL, 23–27 June, 1997. Available from: Biblical Horizons, PO Box 1096, Niceville, FL 32588, USA.

Bonar, A., ed. *Letters of Samuel Rutherford.* Edinburgh: Banner of Truth Trust, 1984.

*Boswell, J., *Christianity, Social Tolerance and Homosexuality.* Chicago: University of Chicago Press, 1980.

*Bradshaw, T., ed. *The Way Forward: Christian Voices on Homosexuality and the Church.* London: Hodder & Stoughton, 1997.

Brooten, B. J. *Love between Women.* Chicago and London: University of Chicago Press, 1996.

Bruce, F. F. *1 and 2 Thessalonians.* Word Biblical Commentary 45. Waco: Word Books, 1982.

Byne, W., et al. "The Interstitial Nuclei of the Human Anterior Hypothalamus: An Investigation of Sexual Variation in Volume and Cell Size, Number and Density." *Brain Research* 856, nos. 1–2 (2000): 254–58.

Byne, W., and B. Parsons. "Human Sexual Orientation: The Biologic Theories Reappraised." *Archives of General Psychiatry* 50 (1993): 228–39.

Byne, W., and E. Stein. "Ethical Implications of Scientific Research on the Causes of Sexual Orientation." *Health Care Analysis* 5, no. 2 (1997): 136–48.

Calvin, J. *Calvin's Commentaries Vol. 11: Romans–Galatians.* Wilmington, DE: Associated Publishers and Authors, n.d.

Clements, R. "Is it Rational to Be Anti-Gay?" http://www.royclements.co.uk/essays17.htm.

—. "How to Avoid the Charge of Homophobia." http://www.royclements.co.uk/essays15.htm.

—. "Why Evangelicals Must Think Again about Homosexuality." http://www.royclements.co.uk/essays08.htm.

Cloninger, C. "A Systematic Method for Clinical Description and Classification of Personality Variants." *Archives of General Psychiatry* 44 (1987): 573–88.

Countryman, W. L., *Dirt, Greed and Sex: Sexual Ethics in the New Testament and Their Implications for Today.* Philadelphia: Fortress Press, 1988.

Cranfield, C. E. B. *A Critical and Exegetical Commentary on the Epistle to the Romans.* International Critical Commentary 1. Edinburgh: T. & T. Clark, 1975.

Deidun, T. J. *New Covenant Morality in Paul.* Rome: Biblical Institute, 1981.

De Young, J. B. *Homosexuality: Contemporary Claims Examined in Light of the Bible and Other Ancient*

*Literature and Law.* Grand Rapids, MI: Kregel Publications, 2000.

Douglas, M. *Purity and Danger: An Analysis of Concepts of Pollution and Taboo.* 2nd ed. London: Routledge & Kegan Paul, 1969.

Dumbrell, W. J. "The Logic of the Role of the Law in Mt. 5:1–20." *Novum Testamentum* 23 (1981): 1–21.

—. *Covenant and Creation: An Old Testament Theology.* Flemington Markets: Lancer; Exeter: Paternoster, 1984.

Dunn, J. D. G. *Romans 1–8.* Word Biblical Commentary 38A. Dallas: Word Books, 1988.

Eckert, E., et al. "Homosexuality in Monozygotic Twins Reared Apart." *British Journal of Psychiatry* 148 (1986): 421–25.

Edwards, B., ed. *Homosexuality: The Straight Agenda.* Epsom: DayOne, 1998.

Fagothey, S. J. *Right and Reason.* 2nd ed. Rockford, IL: Tan, 1959.

Fee, G. D. *The First Epistle to the Corinthians.* New International Commentary on the New Testament. Grand Rapids, MI: Eerdmans, 1987.

—. *God's Empowering Presence: The Holy Spirit in the Letters of Paul.* Peabody, MA: Hendrickson, 1994.

Fisk, B. N. "*porneuein* as Body Violation: The Unique Nature of Sexual Sin in 1 Cor. 6:18." *New Testament Studies* 42 (1996): 540–58.

Foucault, M. *The History of Sexuality: An Introduction.* Translated by R. Hurley. Harmondsworth: Penguin Books, 1978.

*Fox, F. E., and D. W. Virtue. *Homosexuality: Good and Right in the Eyes of God?* Alexandria, VA: Emmaus Ministries, 2002.

Frame, J. *Cornelius Van Til: An Analysis of His Thought.* Phillipsburg, PA: Presbyterian and Reformed, 1995.

Friedman, R. *Male Homosexuality: A Contemporary Psychoanalytical Perspective.* New Haven, CT: Yale University Press, 1988.

*Gagnon, R. A. J. *The Bible and Homosexual Practice: Texts and Hermeneutics.* Nashville: Abingdon, 2001.

—. "The Bible and Homosexual Practice: Theology, Analogies and Genes." *Theology Matters* 7, no. 6 (Nov./Dec. 2001): 4–5.

Gomez, D. W., ed. *True Union in the Body? A Contribution to the Discussion within the Anglican Communion Concerning the Public Blessing of Same-Sex Unions.* Oxford: Future of Anglicanism, 2002.

Goy, R., and B. McEwen. *Sexual Differentiation of the Brain.* Cambridge, MA: MIT Press, 1980.

Green, R. "The Immutability of (Homo)sexual Orientation: Behavioral Science Implications of a Constitutional (Legal) Analysis." *Journal of Psychiatry and Law* (winter 1988): 537–75.

*Greenberg, D. F. *The Construction of Homosexuality.* Chicago and London: University of Chicago Press, 1988.

Hallett, M. "Homosexuality." *Nucleus* (Jan. 1994): 14–19.

Hamer, D., et al. "A Linkage Between DNA Markers on the X Chromosome and Male Sexual Orientation." *Science* 261 (1993): 321–27.

*Hays, R. B. *The Moral Vision of the New Testament.* Edinburgh: T. & T. Clark, 1996.

Jensen, P. "Ordination and the Practice of Homosexuality." In *Faithfulness in Fellowship: Reflections on Homosexuality and the Church.* Papers from the Doctrine Panel of the Anglican Church of Australia. Sydney: John Garratt Publishing, 2001.

*Jenson, R. W. *Systematic Theology.* 2 vols. Oxford: Oxford University Press, 1997, 1999.

Jewett, P. *Who We Are: Our Dignity as Human: A Neo-evangelical Theology.* Grand Rapids, MI: Eerdmans, 1996.

Jewett, R. "The Social Context and Implications of Homoerotic References in Romans." In *Homosexuality, Science, and "the Plain Sense" of Scripture,* edited by D. Balch, 223–41. Grand Rapids, MI: Eerdmans, 2000.

*John, J. *"Permanent, Faithful, Stable" Christian Same-Sex Partnerships.* London: Darton, Longman & Todd, 2000.

Johnson, A., et al. *Sexual Attitudes and Lifestyle.* Oxford: Blackwell Scientific, 1994.

Johnson, A. M., et al. "Sexual Behavior in Britain: Partnerships, Practices, and HIV Risk Behaviors." *The Lancet* 358 (2001): 1835–42.

*Jones, S. L., and M. A Yarhouse. *Homosexuality: The Use of Scientific Research in the Church's Moral Debate.* Downers Grove, IL: InterVarsity Press, 2000.

—. "What Causes Homosexuality?" In *Homosexuality: The Use of Scientific Research in the Church's Moral Debate,* 47–91. Downers Grove, IL: InterVarsity Press, 2000.

Jordan, J. "The Case Against Western Civilization," part 2. *Open Book* 37 (Dec. 1997): http://www.biblical-horizons.com/ob/ob037.htm.

Kallman, F. "Comparative Twin Study of the Genetic Aspects of Homosexuality." *Journal of Nervous and Mental Disease* 115 (1952): 288–98.

*Keane, C., ed. *What Some of You Were: Stories about Christians and Homosexuality.* Sydney and London: Matthias Media, 2001.

Kendler, K. S., et al. "Sexual Orientation in a U.S. National Sample of Twin and Nontwin Sibling Pairs." *American Journal of Psychiatry* 157 (2000): 1843–46.

King, M. "Sexual Orientation and the X." *Nature* 364 (1993): 228–29.

Kinsey, A., et al. *Sexual Behavior in the Human Male.* Philadelphia: W. B. Saunders, 1948.

Kirk, M., and H. Madsen. *After the Ball.* New York: Doubleday, 1989.

Klauber, M. I. "The Helvetic Formula Consensus (1675): An Introduction and Translation." *Trinity Journal* (1990): 103–23.

Landess, T. "Gay Rights in America: The Ultimate PR Campaign." *Rutherford Journal* 3, no. 7 (1994): 3–11.

Lasco, M. S., et al. "A Lack of Dimorphism of Sex or Sexual Orientation in the Human Anterior Commissure." *Brain Research* 936 (2002): 95–98.

Lawton, S. "Key Issues in Counselling Lesbians: Counselling those Struggling with Homosexuality and Lesbianism – A Christian Approach." Lecture from Signposts to Wholeness Conference, True freedom Trust, 1994. Available from TfT at www.truefreedomtrust.co.uk.

LeVay, S. "A Difference in Hypothalamic Structure Between Heterosexual and Homosexual Men." *Science* 253 (1991): 1034–37.

Martin, D. B. *The Corinthian Body.* New Haven: Yale University Press, 1995.

Martin, R. B. *Gerard Manley Hopkins: A Very Private Life.* London: Flamingo, 1992.

Masters, W., and V. Johnson. *Homosexuality in Perspective.* Boston: Little, Brown & Co., 1979.

McCarthy, D. M. "The Relationship of Bodies: A Nuptial Hermeneutic of Same-Sex Unions." In *Theology and Sexuality,* edited by E. F. Rogers, Jr., 200–216. Oxford: Basil Blackwell, 2002.

McGrath, A. E. "Justification." In *Dictionary of Paul and his Letters,* edited by G. F. Hawthorne, R. P. Martin, and D. G. Reid, 517–23. Downers Grove, IL and Leicester: IVP, 1993.

McGuire, T. "Is Homosexuality Genetic? A Critical Review and Some Suggestions." *Journal of Homosexuality* 28, nos. 1–2 (1995): 115–45.

Meyer-Bahlburg, H. "Sex Hormones and Male Homosexuality in Comparative Perspective." *Archives of Sexual Behavior* 6 (1977): 297–325.

—. "Sex Hormones and Female Sexuality: A Critical Examination." *Archives of Sexual Behavior* 8 (1979): 101–19.

—. "Psychoendocrine Research on Sexual Orientation: Current Status and Future Options." *Progress in Brain Research* 61 (1984): 375–98.

Moberley, E. "Homosexuality and the Truth." *First Things* 71 (March 1997): 30–33.

—. "Homosexuality: Structure and Evaluation." *Theology* 83 (1980): 177–84.

Money, J., et al. "Adult Heterosexual Status and Fetal Hormonal Masculinisation." *Psychoneuroendocrinology* 9 (1984): 405–14.

Moo, D. *The Epistle to the Romans.* New International Commentary on the New Testament. Grand Rapids, MI: Eerdmans, 1996.

Muller, J. Z. "Coming Out Ahead: The Homosexual Moment in the Academy." *First Things* 35 (Aug./Sept. 1993): 17–24. Also at http://www.firstthings.com/ftissues/ft9308/articles/muller.html

Muscarella, F. "The Evolution of Homoerotic Behavior in Humans." *Journal of Homosexuality* 40, no. 1 (2000): 51–77.

Neuhaus, R. J. "In the Case of John Boswell." *First Things* 41 (March 1994): 56–59. Also at http://www.first-things.com/ftissues/ft9403/public.html.

Nicolosi, J. "The Gay Deception." In *Homosexuality and American Public Life,* edited by C. Wolfe, 98–105. Dallas: Spence, 1999.

O'Connor, J., and J. Seymour. *Introducing NLP.* London: HarperCollins, 1993.

O'Donovan, O. "Homosexuality in the Church: Can There be a Fruitful Theological Debate?" In *Theology and Sexuality,* edited by E. F. Rogers, Jr., 373–86. Oxford: Basil Blackwell, 2002.

Ovey, M. J. "The Son Incarnate in a Hostile World." In *The Word Became Flesh,* edited by D. Peterson, 50–86. Carlisle: Paternoster, 2003.

Pannenberg, W. "Revelation and Homosexual Experience: What Wolfhart Pannenberg Says about this Debate in the Church." *Christianity Today* 40 (Nov. 11, 1996): 34–37.

Peterson, D. *Possessed by God: A New Testament Theology of Sanctification and Holiness.* New Studies in Biblical Theology 1. Leicester: Apollos; Downers Grove, IL: InterVarsity Press, 1995.

Pillard, R., and M. Bailey. "A Biologic Perspective of Heterosexual, Bisexual and Homosexual Behavior." *Psychiatric Clinics of North America* 18, no. 1 (1995): 71–84.

Plantinga, C. *Not the Way It's Supposed to Be: A Breviary of Sin.* Downers Grove, IL: IVP, 1995.

Punzo, V. C. "Morality and Sexuality." In *Ethics in Practice,* 2nd ed., edited by H. LaFollette, 220–24. Oxford: Basil Blackwell, 2002.

Ramsey Colloquium. "The Homosexual Movement: A Response." *First Things* 41 (March 1994): 15–21. Also at http://www.firstthings.com/ftissues/ft9403/articles/homo.html

Rice, G., et al. "Male Homosexuality: Absence of Linkage to Microsatellite Markers at Xq28." *Science* 284 (1999): 665–67.

*Rogers, E. F., Jr., ed. *Theology and Sexuality.* Oxford: Basil Blackwell, 2002.

Rosner, B. *Paul, Scripture, and Ethics: A Study of 1 Corinthians 5–7.* Leiden: Brill, 1994; Grand Rapids, MI: Baker, 1999.

Rowell, G., K. W. Stevenson, and R. Williams, eds. *Love's Redeeming Work: The Anglican Quest for Holiness.* Oxford: Oxford University Press, 2001.

Rushdoony, R. J. *By What Standard? An Analysis of the Philosophy of Cornelius Van Til.* Philadelphia: Presbyterian and Reformed, 1965.

182                      *Bibliography*

—. *Institutes of Biblical Law,* I. Phillipsburg, PA: Presbyterian and Reformed, 1973.

Saghir, M., and E. Robins. *Male and Female Homosexuality: A Comprehensive Investigation.* Baltimore, MD: Williams Wilkins, 1973.

*Satinover, J. *Homosexuality and the Politics of Truth.* Grand Rapids, MI: Baker, 1996.

—. "The Biology of Homosexuality: Science or Politics?" In *Homosexuality and American Public Life,* edited by C. Wolfe, 3–61. Dallas: Spence, 1999.

Saunders, P. *Homosexuality.* CMF Files 20 (May 2003): 1. http://www.cmf.org.uk/cmffiles/homosex.htm or http://www.cmf.org.uk/cmffiles/pdffiles/homosex.pdf.

—. "Just Genetics?" In *Homosexuality: The Straight Agenda,* edited by B. Edwards, 53–74. Epsom: DayOne, 1998.

Saunders, P., and R. Pickering. "Homosexuality: The Causes." *Nucleus* (Oct. 1997): 19–28.

*Schmidt, T. *Straight and Narrow? Compassion and Clarity in the Homosexuality Debate.* Leicester: IVP, 1995.

—. "The Great Nature-Nurture Debate." In *Straight and Narrow? Compassion and Clarity in the Homosexuality Debate,* 131–59. Leicester: IVP, 1995.

Schuklenk, U., and M. Ristow. "The Ethics of Research into the Cause(s) of Homosexuality." *Journal of Homosexuality* 31, no. 3 (1996): 5–30.

Scroggs, R. *The New Testament and Homosexuality: Contextual Background for Contemporary Debate.* Philadelphia: Fortress Press, 1983.

Seifrid, M. A. *Justification by Faith: The Origin and Development of a Central Pauline Theme.* Brill: Leiden, 1992.

Selbourne, D. *Moral Evasion.* London: Centre for Policy Studies, 1998.

Socarides, C., and B. Kauffman. "Reparative Therapy (letter)." *American Journal of Psychiatry* 151 (1994): 157–59.

South, J. T. *Disciplinary Practices in Pauline Texts.* Lewiston, NY: Edwin Mellen Press, 1992.

Spitzer, R. L. "Can Some Gay Men and Lesbians Change Their Sexual Orientation? 200 Participants Reporting a Change from Homosexual to Heterosexual Orientation." *Archives of Sexual Behavior* 32, no. 5 (2003): 403–17; discussion 419–72.

Swaab, D., and E. Fliers. "A Sexually Dimorphic Nucleus in the Human Brain." *Science* 228 (1985): 1112–14.

Swaab, D., and M. Hoffman. "Sexual Differentiation of the Human Hypothalamus: Ontogeny of the Sexually Dimorphic Nucleus of the Preoptic Area." *Developmental Brain Research* 44 (1988): 314–18.

Thiselton, A. C. *The First Epistle to the Corinthians: A Commentary on the Greek Text.* New International Greek Testament Commentary. Grand Rapids, MI: Eerdmans; Carlisle: Paternoster, 2000.

Thompson, L. "Search for a Gay Gene." *Time* (12 June 1995): 52–53.

Thornton, B. S. *Eros: The Myth of Ancient Greek Sexuality.* Oxford: Westview, 1997.

Tonks, A. "British Sex Survey Shows Popularity of Monogamy." *British Medical Journal* 308 (1994): 209.

Townsend, C. "Homosexuality: Finding the Way of Truth and Love." In *Christianity in a Changing World*, edited by M. Schluter and M. Ovey, 23–25. London: Marshall Pickering, 2000.

Van Til, C. *The Defense of the Faith.* Rev. ed. Philadelphia: Presbyterian and Reformed, 1963.

—. *A Christian Theory of Knowledge.* Nutley, NJ: Presbyterian and Reformed, 1969.

Van Wyk, P., and C. Geist. "Psychosocial Development of Heterosexual, Bisexual and Homosexual Behavior." *Archives of Sexual Behavior* 13 (1984): 505–44.

*Vasey, M. *Strangers and Friends.* London: Hodder & Stoughton, 1995.

Wallace, D. B. *Greek Grammar Beyond the Basics.* Grand Rapids, MI: Zondervan, 1996.

Webb, B. G. "Homosexuality in Scripture." In *Theological and Pastoral Responses to Homosexuality Explorations 8,* edited by B. G. Webb, 65–104. Adelaide: Openbook, 1994.

Wenham, G. J. *The Book of Leviticus.* New International Commentary on the Old Testament. Grand Rapids, MI: Eerdmans, 1979.

—. "The Old Testament Attitude to Homosexuality." *Expository Times* 102 (1991): 359–63.

Whyte, A. *Samuel Rutherford and Some of His Correspondents.* Edinburgh: Oliphant Anderson & Ferrier, 1894.

Williams, G. J. *The Theology of Rowan Williams: An Outline, Critique and Consideration of its Consequences.* Latimer Studies. London: Latimer Trust, 2002.

*Williams, R. *The Body's Grace.* 2nd ed. London: Lesbian and Gay Christian Movement and The Institute for the Study of Christianity and Sexuality, 2002. Also reprinted in Rogers (ed.), *Theology and Sexuality,* 309–21.

Wold, D. *Out of Order: Homosexuality in the Bible and the Ancient Near East.* Grand Rapids, MI: Baker, 1998.

*Wolfe, C., ed. *Homosexuality and American Public Life.* Dallas: Spence, 1999.

—. ed. *Same-Sex Matters: The Challenge of Homosexuality.* Dallas: Spence, 2000.

Wright, D. F. "Homosexuals or Prostitutes? The Meaning of *arsenokoitēs* (1 Cor. 6:9; 1 Tim. 1:10)," *Vigiliae Christianae* 38 (1984): 125–53.

—. "Translating *arsenokoitai* (1 Cor. 6:9; 1 Tim. 1:10)," *Vigiliae Christianae* 41 (1987): 396–98.

Wright, J. R. "Boswell on Homosexuality: A Case Undemonstrated." *Anglican Theological Review* LXVI (1984): 79–94.

# Notes

1 Cf. C. Keane, ed., *What Some of You Were: Stories about Christians and Homosexuality* (Sydney and London: Matthias Media, 2001), for a series of other testimonies of a similar character.

2 The web site is www.truefreedomtrust.co.uk. TfT offers counseling, support groups, literature, tapes, speakers, and seminars.

3 G. J. Wenham, "The Old Testament Attitude to Homosexuality," *ExpTim* 102 (1991): 359–63 (p. 363).

4 This is a summary of the argument of R. A. J. Gagnon, "The Bible and Homosexual Practice: Theology, Analogies and Genes," *Theology Matters* 7, no. 6 (Nov./Dec. 2001): 4–5.

5 *The Body's Grace*, 2nd ed. (London: Lesbian and Gay Christian Movement and The Institute for the Study of Christianity and Sexuality, 2002). Also reprinted in E. F. Rogers, Jr., ed., *Theology and Sexuality* (Oxford: Basil Blackwell, 2002), 309–21.

6 Cf. G. Rowell, K. W. Stevenson, and R. Williams, eds., *Love's Redeeming Work: The Anglican Quest for Holiness* (Oxford: OUP, 2001). The index of this anthology, covering about five hundred years of Anglican thinking on holiness, contains no reference to the body or sexuality or chastity. This omission is surprising, given the link between these ideas in Scripture and in Christian teaching about holiness across the centuries.

7  "Just as a priest is separated from an ancient society in order to serve it and serves it by his distinctiveness, so Israel serves her world by maintaining her distance and her difference from it" (W. J. Dumbrell, *Covenant and Creation: An Old Testament Theology* [Flemington Markets: Lancer; Exeter: Paternoster, 1984], 90). Dumbrell provides an excellent discussion of Exod. 19:5–6, showing particularly how Israel was to exercise an "Abrahamic role" (pp. 84–90).

8  Cf. G. J. Wenham, *The Book of Leviticus*, NICOT (Grand Rapids, MI: Eerdmans, 1979), 5. Note Wenham's examination of holiness and purity in Leviticus (pp. 18–25).

9  Wenham, *Leviticus*, 251.

10  The noun *tô'ēbâ* ("abomination") is related to the verb *t'b* ("abhor, detest"). In the OT, "pagan worship practices, deceit and insubordination within the covenant nation, and superficial worship of Yahweh constitute three major realms of abhorrent activities" (M. A. Grisanti, *NIDOTTE* 4:315).

11  W. C. Williams, *NIDOTTE* 4:102, overstates the case when he concludes that, "when used to denote sexual relations, the idiom 'lie with' and its derivatives denote sexual relations that are illicit." Exceptions such as Gen. 30:15–16; 2 Sam. 11:11; 12:24 show that the expression can be used of legitimate sexual relations.

12  Wenham, "*Homosexuality*," 361.

13  Wenham, "*Homosexuality*," 363.

14  Wenham, "*Homosexuality*," 363. Leviticus refers to incest as, literally, sex with your "own flesh" (18:16–17; 20:19). Homosexuality is similarly rejected because it involves intercourse between beings that are too much alike. By contrast, bestiality is condemned because it is sex between beings that are too much unlike. Note that Lev. 18:23 condemns bestiality because it is literally "a confusion" (Heb. *tebel* from *bālal*, "to mix"; EVV "perversion"). Cf. 20:12, where the same word is used in connection with a man having intercourse with his daughter-in-law.

[15] M. Douglas, *Purity and Danger: An Analysis of Concepts of Pollution and Taboo*, 2nd ed. (London: Routledge & Kegan Paul, 1969), 54.

[16] B. G. Webb, "Homosexuality in Scripture," in *Theological and Pastoral Responses to Homosexuality Explorations 8*, ed. B. G. Webb (Adelaide: Openbook, 1994), 65–104 (p. 82).

[17] Webb, "Homosexuality in Scripture," 82.

[18] Wenham, *Leviticus*, 284–86. Wenham argues that the penalties prescribed in the law were the maximum penalties. Where there were mitigating circumstances, lesser penalties would have been enforced. "Cutting off" is "a threat of direct punishment by God usually in the form of premature death."

[19] Cf. Webb, "Homosexuality in Scripture," 83–84.

[20] W. J. Dumbrell, "The Logic of the Role of the Law in Mt. 5:1–20," *NovT* 23 (1981): 1–21 (p. 19).

[21] R. J. Banks, *Jesus and the Law in the Synoptic Tradition*, SNTSMS 28 (Cambridge: CUP, 1975), 141. Contravention of the Mosaic law at this point is unlikely, since Jesus has just argued from the law about the invalidity of Pharisaical traditions.

[22] R. A. J. Gagnon, *The Bible and Homosexual Practice: Texts and Hermeneutics* (Nashville: Abingdon, 2001), 191. Consistent with OT teaching, Jewish writers who were roughly contemporary with Jesus condemned homosexual practice as a violation of God's will (e.g., Wis. 14:26; T. Levi 17:11; Sib. Or. 3:596–600; Philo, *Spec. Laws* 3.39; Josephus, *Ag. Ap.* 2.273). It is impossible to imagine that Jesus thought or taught otherwise.

[23] Webb, "Homosexuality in Scripture," 85. Gagnon, *The Bible and Homosexual Practice*, 197, argues that Jesus' expectations regarding sexual purity, "in some respects at least, exceeded the expectations both of the Torah and of the traditions prevailing in Jesus' day."

[24] D. W. Gomez, ed., *True Union in the Body? A Contribution to the Discussion within the Anglican Communion Concerning the Public Blessing of Same-Sex Unions* (Oxford: Future of Anglicanism, 2002), 11.

[25] Gagnon, *The Bible and Homosexual Practice*, 228. The argument that Jesus was neutral or even affirming of homosexual conduct is "revisionist history."

[26] Gomez, ed., *True Union in the Body?*, 23.

[27] Proposition 2 of Six Propositions from the Inter-Anglican Theological and Doctrinal Commission, 2003.

[28] The noun *hagiasmos* in 4:3, 4, 7 could be understood as a synonym for "holiness" in 3:13 (*hagiōsynē*), meaning the state or condition to which we are called in Christ. However, it is possible that a more dynamic sense should be understood. God's will is "sanctification" in the sense that he demands a consecrated lifestyle. We are to keep our bodies sanctified for him (4:4) because that is the context, or condition, in which we were called (4:7). Cf. D. Peterson, *Possessed by God: A New Testament Theology of Sanctification and Holiness*, NSBT 1 (Leicester: Apollos; Downers Grove, IL: InterVarsity Press, 1995), 139–42.

[29] Cf. BAGD, 693; Grimm-Thayer, 531–2. H. Reisser, *NIDNTT* 1:497, argues that the Greek word group can describe various modes of extramarital sex "insofar as they deviate from accepted social and religious norms (e.g., homosexuality, promiscuity, paedophilia, and especially prostitution)."

[30] "To control your own body" is the rendering of the Greek *to heautou skeuos ktasthai* preferred by NRSV, NIV, ESV. Cf. F. F. Bruce, *1 and 2 Thessalonians*, WBC 45 (Waco: Word Books, 1982), 83. The word *skeuos* literally means "thing, object, vessel," but it is used figuratively in various ways. E. Best, *A Commentary on the First and Second Epistles to the Thessalonians*, BNTC (London: A. & C. Black, 1977), 161–63, takes it to mean "wife" in 1 Thess. 4:4, as do NRSV and ESV margins ("to take a wife for himself"), and NIV margin ("to live with his own wife").

[31] The reasons for such an approach are well presented, and then dismissed, by Best, *Thessalonians*, 165–66. He rightly points out

that this verse could be referring specifically to homosexual exploitation of a fellow Christian.

[32] "The dynamic that makes Paul's argument against sexual impurity possible is the experienced reality of the Spirit" (G. D. Fee, *God's Empowering Presence: The Holy Spirit in the Letters of Paul* [Peabody, MA: Hendrickson, 1994], 53).

[33] This is another way of speaking about God's law being written on the heart (Jer. 31:33). The Thessalonians' love for one another is "the effect of God's immediate and efficacious action at the very source of their moral personality" (T. J. Deidun, *New Covenant Morality in Paul* [Rome: Biblical Institute, 1981], 58).

[34] Deidun, *New Covenant Morality*, 58. In the holy people of the new covenant, "the consecrating and unifying power of God's presence is interiorised," 60.

[35] A. C. Thiselton, *The First Epistle to the Corinthians: A Commentary on the Greek Text*, NIGTC (Grand Rapids, MI: Eerdmans; Carlisle: Paternoster, 2000), 381.

[36] Thiselton, *First Epistle to the Corinthians*, 397 (emphasis removed). Thiselton argues against the view that "the flesh" to be destroyed is the person's human body. Cf. J. T. South, *Disciplinary Practices in Pauline Texts* (Lewiston, NY: Edwin Mellen Press, 1992), 1–88, 181–98.

[37] K. Bailey, "Paul's Theological Foundation for Human Sexuality: 1 Cor. 6:12–20 in the Light of Rhetorical Criticism," *NETR* 3 (1980): 27–41, argues that the sexual issues relate to 5:1–13 and 6:12–20; and the issues of greed and grasping, eating and being drunk to 11:17–34.

[38] Thiselton, *First Epistle to the Corinthians*, 447 (emphasis removed), concluding a whole section of interaction with alternative views (pp. 440–47).

[39] Cf. G. D. Fee, *The First Epistle to the Corinthians*, NICNT (Grand Rapids, MI: Eerdmans, 1987), 243–44, interacting with R. Scroggs, *The New Testament and Homosexuality: Contextual Background for Contemporary Debate* (Philadelphia: Fortress Press, 1983) and J. Boswell, *Christianity,*

*Social Tolerance and Homosexuality* (Chicago: University of
Chicago Press, 1980). Gagnon, *The Bible and Homosexual
Practice*, 308–12, argues that *malakoi* in 1 Cor. 6:9 refers to
immoral sexual intercourse, rather than effeminate behavior,
because it is sandwiched in between the terms *moichoi* and
*arsenokoitai*.

⁴⁰ Boswell, *Christianity, Social Tolerance and Homosexuality*,
345–53.

⁴¹ Boswell, *Christianity, Social Tolerance and Homosexuality*,
105.

⁴² Cf. Scroggs, *The New Testament and Homosexuality*, 106ff.;
J. R. Wright, "Boswell on Homosexuality: A Case
Undemonstrated," *AThR* LXVI (1984): 79–94; D. F. Wright,
"Homosexuals or Prostitutes? The Meaning of *arsenokoitēs* (1
Cor. 6:9; 1 Tim. 1:10)," *VC* 38 (1984): 125–53; "Translating
*arsenokoitai* (1 Cor. 6:9; 1 Tim. 1:10)," *VC* 41 (1987): 396–98.

⁴³ Cf. Gagnon, *The Bible and Homosexual Practice*, 312–36, critiquing Scroggs and others.

⁴⁴ Cf. Webb, "Homosexuality in Scripture," 92; Thiselton, *First
Epistle to the Corinthians*, 448–52.

⁴⁵ B. Rosner, *Paul, Scripture, and Ethics: A Study of 1 Corinthians
5–7* (Leiden: Brill, 1994; Grand Rapids, MI: Baker, 1999), 120.

⁴⁶ Fee, *First Epistle to the Corinthians*, 245.

⁴⁷ C. K. Barrett, *A Commentary on the First Epistle to the
Corinthians*, 2nd ed. (London: A. & C. Black, 1971), 141, points
out that the use of the non-technical *apelousasthe*, instead of
*ebaptisthēte* ("you were baptized"), implies that "it is the inward
meaning rather than the outward circumstances of the rite that
is important to Paul." Fee, *First Epistle to the Corinthians*,
246–47, is less certain about baptismal associations in 1 Cor.
6:11. Nevertheless, he still equates "washing" with regeneration
through the Spirit, which is inconsistent with his view that the
metaphor refers to the removal of "the 'filth' of the vice catalogue" in vv. 9–10, in which case it is another way of talking
about forgiveness.

[48] In the apostolic preaching, the offer of forgiveness is directly linked with repentance towards God and faith in Jesus as the Christ (cf. Acts 2:38; 3:19–20; 5:31; 10:43; 13:38–39). Baptism is not always explicitly mentioned in this connection, although it is regularly associated with commitment to Christ and the beginning of the Christian life.

[49] A. E. McGrath, "Justification," in *Dictionary of Paul and his Letters*, ed. G. F. Hawthorne, R. P. Martin, and D. G. Reid (Downers Grove, IL and Leicester: IVP, 1993), 517–23 (p. 518). Cf. M. A. Seifrid, *Justification by Faith: The Origin and Development of a Central Pauline Theme* (Brill: Leiden, 1992).

[50] Barrett, *First Epistle to the Corinthians*, 142. He argues that Paul is referring to "the moral effects of conversion" *in us*, rooted in the work of Christ *outside of us* and *for us*, and "sealed in baptism."

[51] *Calvin's Commentaries Vol. 11: Romans–Galatians* (Wilmington, DE: Associated Publishers and Authors, n.d.), 1602.

[52] Fee, *God's Empowering Presence*, 129. Fee rightly opposes the view that each verb in the sequence corresponds to the persons of the Trinity (washed = Christ; sanctified = Spirit; justified = God).

[53] Rosner, *Paul, Scripture, and Ethics*, 118, rightly observes that "the same structure of thought (identity informs behavior) pervades the book of Deuteronomy and is scattered throughout the Hebrew prophets."

[54] We must continue to see ourselves as God sees us in Christ. G. C. Berkouwer, *Faith and Sanctification* (Grand Rapids, MI: Eerdmans, 1952), 21, observes that, "The moment sanctification is ejected from the temple of faith, and hence of justification, that moment justification by faith has become an initial stage on the pilgrim's journey, a supply-station which later becomes a pleasant memory."

[55] Thiselton, *First Epistle to the Corinthians*, 459. Thiselton, pp. 462–63, rightly proposes that the second slogan included the

words "and God will destroy both one and the other" (v. 13), which are usually not included in the quotation marks in English versions.

56  Fee, *First Epistle to the Corinthians*, 251.

57  Thiselton, *First Epistle to the Corinthians*, 462. Thiselton notes that "this becomes even more marked if proto-gnostic influences were also at work." Cf. Barrett, *First Epistle to the Corinthians*, 144–45, on the different directions that Gnosticism took.

58  Barrett, *First Epistle to the Corinthians*, 147 (emphasis removed). Paul opposes the view that there is a valid analogy between the use of the stomach for digestion and of the body for fornication. "Sexual intercourse, unlike eating, is an act of the whole person, and therefore participates not in the transiency of material members but in the continuity of the resurrection life" (p. 148).

59  Thiselton, *First Epistle to the Corinthians*, 464. Thiselton brings out clearly the corporate or communal dimension to this idea. It links with the biblical emphasis on an appropriate love between the redeemed – a love which does not cross forbidden boundaries.

60  Fee, *First Epistle to the Corinthians*, 258. The present implication of this is that the public embodied life of Christ's people is "the instantiation of the gospel which points to, and thereby identifies Christ for the world" (Thiselton, *First Epistle to the Corinthians*, 466).

61  D. B. Martin, *The Corinthian Body* (New Haven: Yale University Press, 1995), 228. Thiselton, *First Epistle to the Corinthians*, 468, observes that, "The identity crisis which the immoral relationship brings about concerns both the individual identity boundaries of the offender and the corporate identity boundaries of what it is to belong to the people of Christ in union with Christ."

62  So Fee, *First Epistle to the Corinthians*, 260, and Thiselton, *First Epistle to the Corinthians*, 469.

[63] Thiselton, *First Epistle to the Corinthians*, 471–72, lists and comments on the alternative views. Fee, *First Epistle to the Corinthians*, 261–63, seriously entertains the possibility that it is a Corinthian slogan which Paul develops but then argues against this position.

[64] B. N. Fisk, "*porneuein* as Body Violation: The Unique Nature of Sexual Sin in 1 Cor. 6:18," *NTS* 42 (1996): 540–58 (p. 557).

[65] Thiselton, *First Epistle to the Corinthians*, 474. Cf. D. S. Bailey, *The Man-Woman Relation in Christian Thought* (London: Longmans, Green, 1959), 9–10.

[66] Fee, *First Epistle to the Corinthians*, 266.

[67] Gomez, ed., *True Union in the Body?*, 24. "Following the example of Jesus, the New Testament Church welcomed all, relativizing the distinctions between Jew and Gentile, whilst at the same time preserving a distinctive ethical challenge" (p. 25).

[68] Gomez, ed., *True Union in the Body?*, 3.

[69] A brief summary and critique of this position is provided by G. J. Williams, *The Theology of Rowan Williams: An Outline, Critique and Consideration of its Consequences*, Latimer Studies (London: Latimer Trust, 2002), 30–37.

[70] *The Body's Grace*, 11.

[71] *The Body's Grace*, 12.

[72] Gagnon, *The Bible and Homosexual Practice*.

[73] Gomez, ed., *True Union in the Body?*, 29.

[74] See, e.g., the discussion of this verse in Chapter 2, above.

[75] J. John, *"Permanent, Faithful, Stable" Christian Same-Sex Partnerships* (London: Darton, Longman & Todd, 2000), 3. He quite legitimately raises the question about the way the Bible has been handled in Anglican debates about the remarriage of divorcees and the ordination of women to the priesthood.

[76] John, *"Permanent, Faithful, Stable,"* 4.

[77] John, *"Permanent, Faithful, Stable,"* 4.

[78] "The Form of Solemnization of Matrimony" in *The Book of Common Prayer* (1662).

[79] John, *"Permanent, Faithful, Stable,"* 11–12.

[80] John, *"Permanent, Faithful, Stable,"* 13.

[81] B. S. Thornton, *Eros: The Myth of Ancient Greek Sexuality* (Oxford: Westview, 1997), xi. Thornton offers a strong challenge to views that the Greeks regarded homosexual relationships as normal and good, that the Greeks approved the practice of pederasty, and that the Greeks regarded married sex as being for procreation, rather than loving union. I am grateful to Archbishop Peter Jensen for pointing me to relevant literature on this subject. Cf. P. Jensen, "Ordination and the Practice of Homosexuality," in *Faithfulness in Fellowship: Reflections on Homosexuality and the Church*, Papers from the Doctrine Panel of the Anglican Church of Australia (Sydney: John Garratt Publishing, 2001), 161–80.

[82] D. F. Greenberg, *The Construction of Homosexuality* (Chicago and London: University of Chicago Press, 1988), 485.

[83] B. J. Brooten, *Love between Women* (Chicago and London: University of Chicago Press, 1996), 144.

[84] Brooten, *Love between Women*, 233. While she is impelled by the evidence to agree that Paul condemns all same-sex practices, whatever the disposition involved, it is sad that she nevertheless expresses the hope that churches today "will no longer teach Rom. 1:26f. as authoritative" (p. 302).

[85] John, *"Permanent, Faithful, Stable,"* 14.

[86] Cf. J. D. G. Dunn, *Romans 1–8*, WBC 38A (Dallas: Word, 1988), 53, 61. Dunn notes the universal appeal of the argument but says that "in v21 and overwhelmingly from v23 onward Paul speaks as a Jew and makes use of the standard Hellenistic Jewish polemic against idolatry."

[87] D. Moo, *The Epistle to the Romans*, NICNT (Grand Rapids, MI: Eerdmans, 1996), 92.

[88] Paul uses the same verb (*edoxasan*), translated "honor" in Rom. 1:21, as he uses in 1 Cor. 6:20, where it is translated "glorify."

[89] English versions rightly translate the aorist tense of the Greek verbs in 1:18–32 with the English past tense (hence "exchanged" in v. 23). However, it would be wrong to conclude that the

reference is simply to some action in the past, such as the fall of humanity recorded in Genesis 3, or even the fall of Israel into idolatry in Exodus 32 (suggested by the use of language echoing Ps. 106:20 LXX). The aorists in this passage are "consummative," or even "gnomic," describing what is generally true of human experience. Cf. D. B. Wallace, *Greek Grammar Beyond the Basics* (Grand Rapids, MI: Zondervan, 1996), 559–62.

[90] C. E. B. Cranfield, *A Critical and Exegetical Commentary on the Epistle to the Romans*, ICC 1 (Edinburgh: T. & T. Clark, 1975), 121, suggests that "God allowed them to go their own way in order that they might at last learn from their consequent wretchedness to hate the futility of a life turned away from the truth of God." Gagnon, *The Bible and Homosexual Practice*, 252–53, helpfully outlines five stages in "exchanges" and "giving overs" in Paul's argument.

[91] Dunn, *Romans 1–8*, 64.

[92] Cf. Cranfield, *Romans*, 125–26. For this appeal to "nature" in the sense of the order manifest in the created world, Cranfield compares 1 Cor. 11:14. Dunn, *Romans 1–8*, 64, notes that "nature" is not a Hebrew but a Greek concept, typically Stoic. However, the idea of living in harmony with God's created order and his purposes is certainly Jewish. Cf. Wis. 13–14; *T. Naph.* 3:4–5.

[93] Gagnon, *The Bible and Homosexual Practice*, 254, in the light of his extensive chap. 2.

[94] NRSV translates Rom. 2:14 "instinctively" and Gal. 2:15 "by birth."

[95] M. Vasey, *Strangers and Friends* (London: Hodder & Stoughton, 1995), 13; Scroggs, *The New Testament and Homosexuality*, 109–18.

[96] John, *"Permanent, Faithful, Stable,"* 15.

[97] Cf. Cranfield, *Romans*, 125. Two Jewish writers roughly contemporary with Paul, both Philo (*Spec. Laws* 3.39) and Josephus (*Ag. Ap.* 2.273), use the expression *para physin* in connection with homosexual intercourse and God's purpose in creation.

98 Cf. Matt. 5:27–30; Col. 3:5–7. Gagnon, *The Bible and Homosexual Practice*, 264, argues that Paul singles out same-sex intercourse because "it represents one of the clearest instances of conscious suppression of revelation in nature by gentiles, inasmuch as it involves denying clear and anatomical differences and functions (leaving them 'without excuse')."

99 Gomez, ed., *True Union in the Body?*, 26.

100 Gagnon, *The Bible and Homosexual Practice*, 239, notes that the LXX use of this noun in Lev. 18:6–19; 20:11, 17–21, is another possible indication that Paul is alluding to the Levitical background. It could thus be understood as "indecent exposure and intercourse."

101 Cranfield, *Romans*, 126–27. Moo, *Romans*, 116, suggests that "this could be a vivid way of saying that those who engage in such activities will suffer eternal punishment; they will receive 'in their own persons' God's penalty for violation of his will." Cf. Gagnon, *The Bible and Homosexual Practice*, 260–63.

102 Gagnon, *The Bible and Homosexual Practice*, 286.

103 Gagnon, *The Bible and Homosexual Practice*, 291.

104 R. B. Hays, *The Moral Vision of the New Testament* (Edinburgh: T. & T. Clark, 1996), 402.

105 Gagnon, *The Bible and Homosexual Practice*.

106 Gagnon, *The Bible and Homosexual Practice*, 37.

107 Gagnon, *The Bible and Homosexual Practice*, 487. See pp. 487–89 for a fuller summary.

108 Hays, *Moral Vision*, 394.

109 W. Pannenberg, "Revelation and Homosexual Experience: What Wolfhart Pannenberg Says about this Debate in the Church," *Christianity Today* 40 (Nov. 11, 1996): 34–37 (p. 37).

110 Richard Neuhaus, writing in C. Wolfe, ed., *Homosexuality and American Public Life* (Dallas: Spence, 1999), 247.

111 J. Satinover, *Homosexuality and the Politics of Truth* (Grand Rapids, MI: Baker, 1996), 18.

112 The Ramsay Colloquium, named after Paul Ramsay, is a group of Jewish and Christian theologians, ethicists, philosophers,

and scholars that meets periodically to consider questions of morality, religion, and public life.

[113] "The Homosexual Movement: A Response," *First Things* 41 (March 1994): 15–21. Also at http://www.firstthings.com/ftissues/ft9403/articles/homo.html.

[114] R. W. Jenson, *Systematic Theology* (Oxford: OUP, 1997, 1999), 2:133.

[115] Interestingly, this accords with Eugene Rogers' characterization of Rowan Williams' form of argument in *The Body's Grace*. See Rogers, ed., *Theology and Sexuality*, 218–19, 309. The deliberate adoption of such a method, then, does not of itself constitute a breach of the rules of argument upon matters relating to homosexuality as suggested by Oliver O'Donovan in his article in the same book (p. 374) and by Roy Clements in his essays "Is it Rational to Be Anti-Gay?" (http://www.royclements.co.uk/essays17.htm) and "How to Avoid the Charge of Homophobia" (http://www.royclements.co.uk/essays15.htm).

[116] The radical amoralism of Foucault, for example, only serves to confirm this point. Jerry Z. Muller ("Coming Out Ahead: The Homosexual Moment in the Academy," *First Things* 35 (Aug./Sept. 1993): 17–24 [also at http://www.firstthings.com/ftissues/ft9403/articles/homo.html]) writes: "Foucault's writings span a remarkable range of topics, from the rise of mental institutions, prisons, and academic disciplines such as political economy and linguistics, to conceptions of sexuality. Yet his works are unified by an underlying theme: 'It could be otherwise.' In his writings on each of these topics, Foucault undertook to trace the genealogy of one or another conception of 'normalcy,' with the aim of demonstrating that what we take to be standards of normalcy are merely historical and, by implication, arbitrary constructs."

[117] Westminster Shorter Catechism, question 14.

[118] It is unsurprising that biblically regulated taxonomies of sin take distinctively *theological* shape. Although he makes no such claim for it, Robert Jenson's threefold/fourfold taxonomy of sin

as idolatry-unbelief, lust-injustice, and despair, takes Trinitarian form: the sin of idolatry-unbelief against the Father, the sin of injustice-lust against the brother-son, and the sin of despair against the eschatological Spirit.

119 Jenson, *Systematic Theology*, 2:137.

120 It is to be expected, therefore, that opposition to "true religion" will often take "religious" form. It is interesting that Michel Foucault should describe the reaction against "the monotonous nights of the Victorian bourgeoisie" in this way: "A great sexual sermon – which has had its subtle theologians and its popular voices – has swept through our societies over the last decades; it has chastised the old order, denounced hypocrisy, and praised the rights of the immediate and the real; it has made people dream of a New City" (*The History of Sexuality: An Introduction*, trans. R. Hurley [Harmondsworth: Penguin Books, 1978], 7–8). Not that Foucault approves of this sermon, for it, like the one it drowns out, is an exercise of power in defining and declaring what is good and what is evil. Anxiously trying to discover which sermon is currently found most persuasive reveals the "irony . . . of believing that our 'liberation' is in the balance" (159).

121 Cf. M. J. Ovey, "The Son Incarnate in a Hostile World," in *The Word Became Flesh*, ed. D. Peterson (Carlisle: Paternoster, 2003), 50–86.

122 "As we deny our end in God, so does the world, which was made to enable this end, lose its meaning" (Jenson, *Systematic Theology*, 2:152).

123 "The Homosexual Movement: A Response."

124 Hays, *Moral Vision*, 388.

125 The literature upon the significance of the phrase and the concept "the image of God" is immense. Standard theological dictionaries and encyclopedia provide surveys of the debate and almost overwhelming bibliographical leads.

126 In Romans 1, of course, the idea of "exchange" lies at the heart of Paul's charge. Sinners exchange the glory of God for idols

(v. 23), exchange the truth of God for a lie (v. 25), and exchange natural sexual relations for unnatural ones (v. 26). See the discussion of Romans 1 in Chapter 3, above, as well as Robert Jewett's comments on "exchange" in "The Social Context and Implications of Homoerotic References in Romans," in *Homosexuality, Science, and "the Plain Sense" of Scripture*, ed. D. Balch (Grand Rapids, MI: Eerdmans, 2000), 223–41 (esp. pp. 226, 231).

[127] This is an implication, too, of the understanding that if evil is *privatio boni* (the privation, absence, or loss of the good), then unlimited and unadulterated evil is impossible.

[128] I take it that the God-hater's tension is not resolved in the lake of fire because such a resolution would require the complete obliteration of the image of God. This would raise two problems. First, for personal continuity: is the person being punished truly the person who committed the sin? Second, for personal consciousness: with the image of God obliterated, is a reflective and self-conscious understanding of punishment possible? Those in the lake of fire would be ex-humans rather than humans.

[129] It is intriguing how closely Foucault's concluding analysis in *The History of Sexuality* (pp.155–56) matches this. He writes "It is through sex – in fact, an imaginary point determined by the deployment of sexuality – that each individual has to pass in order to have access to his own intelligibility . . . to the whole of his body . . . to his identity. Through a reversal that doubtless had its surreptitious beginnings long ago . . . we have arrived at the point where we expect our intelligibility to come from what was for many centuries thought of as madness; the plenitude of our body from what was long considered its stigma and likened to a wound; our identity from what was perceived as an obscure and nameless urge. Hence the importance we ascribe to it, the reverential fear with which we surround it, the care we take to know it. Hence the fact that over the centuries it has become more important than our soul, more

important almost than our life; and so it is that all the world's enigmas appear frivolous to us compared to this secret, miniscule in each of us, but of a density that makes it more serious than any other. The Faustian pact, whose temptation has been instilled in us by the deployment of sexuality, is now as follows: to exchange life in its entirety for sex itself, for the truth and sovereignty of sex. Sex is worth dying for. It is in this (strictly historical) sense that sex is indeed imbued with the death instinct. When a long while ago the West discovered love, it bestowed on it a value high enough to make death acceptable; nowadays it is sex that claims this equivalence, the highest of all. And while the deployment of sexuality permits the techniques of power to invest life, the fictitious point of sex, itself marked by that deployment, exerts enough charm on everyone for them to accept hearing the grumble of death within it." This analysis requires redirection rather than denial. With reference to disordered sex, and particularly same-sex sexual acts, what Foucault attributes to sex is indeed an endeavor to do away with God: sex is true, sovereign, and worth dying for. In terms of the current analysis, Foucault's "intelligibility" is truth, his "identity" is life, his "access to the whole of his body" is love, and the "reversal" he describes is to take sinful sex and use it as a weapon against and a substitute for the real God.

130 Foucault, *History of Sexuality*, 135, 138.
131 See, for example, Satinover, *Homosexuality*, and F. E. Fox and D. W. Virtue, *Homosexuality: Good and Right in the Eyes of God?* (Alexandria, VA: Emmaus Ministries, 2002).
132 Contra Williams, *The Body's Grace*.
133 Muller, "Coming Out Ahead."
134 Hays, *Moral Vision*, 388.
135 Jenson, *Systematic Theology*, 2:146.
136 J. Jordan, "The Case Against Western Civilization," part 2, *Open Book* 37 (Dec. 1997). Also at: http://www.biblicalhorizons.com/ob/ob037.htm.

137 R. Clements, "Why Evangelicals Must Think Again about Homosexuality," http://www.royclements.co.uk/essays08.htm.

138 "The Homosexual Movement: A Response."

139 Roy Clements goes on to employ this sort of argument in "Why Evangelicals."

140 Jenson, *Systematic Theology*, 2:139.

141 Jenson, *Systematic Theology*, 2:140.

142 Jenson, *Systematic Theology*, 2:140.

143 Jenson, *Systematic Theology*, 2:141.

144 D. M. McCarthy ("The Relationship of Bodies: A Nuptial Hermeneutic of Same-Sex Unions," in *Theology and Sexuality*, ed. Rogers, 200–216) claims that "A homosexual orientation, properly understood, is this: gay men and lesbians are persons who encounter the other (and thus discover themselves) in relation to persons of the same sex" and that this is how the "nuptial meaning of life" emerges for gay men and lesbians (pp. 212–13). This is disingenuous: to speak of "nuptial meaning" and then to claim that "homosexual and heterosexual desire follow along the same path insofar as both seek fulfillment through difference" empties the account of the separate and distinct creation of woman of its significance.

145 "The Homosexual Movement: A Response."

146 Jenson, *Systematic Theology*, 2:141.

147 R. Bledsoe, "Envy, Scapegoating and Neurosis," a series of addresses at the Biblical Horizons Conference, Niceville, FL, 23–27 June, 1997.

148 Muller, "Coming Out Ahead."

149 Cited by Jenson, *Systematic Theology*, 2:89.

150 Jenson, *Systematic Theology*, 2:92; and V. C. Punzo, "Morality and Sexuality," in *Ethics in Practice*, ed. H. LaFollette, 2nd ed., 220–24 (Oxford: Basil Blackwell, 2002).

151 Gagnon, *The Bible and Homosexual Practice*, 37.

152 Rejection of heterosexual married love is, of course, different from the call to singleness – whether that call is experienced as vocation or frustration. Additionally, Jenson's point is related:

"Homoeroticism is of course not a mode of sexuality at all, but an escape from it. Homoeroticism is a group of sensual techniques, devised to abstract sexuality's pleasure without commitment to its function" (*Systematic Theology*, 2:93). Here the "function" of sexuality is that of final commitment rather than the bearing of children.

[153] The "body's grace" then will move from God's pleasure with what Jesus did in the "body" prepared for him (Heb. 10) through Jesus taking our sin in his "body" on the tree (1 Pet. 2:24), thus having his "body" broken for us (1 Cor. 11:24). By the Spirit's work of grace we will be made members of the "body" of Christ (1 Cor. 12:13), so that as the objects of God's love we will seek to glorify God in our "bodies" (1 Cor. 6:20). We will thereby find ourselves reconciled to those we previously hated, as well as to God, in the one "body" of Christ through the cross. Rowan Williams states that "We are pleased because we are pleasing" ("The Body's Grace," 313), but, although this is true, it is transcended by that to which, rightly understood, it points. "We love because he first loved us" (1 John 4:19). So far as our desires and acts are contrary to the law of God, which is the law of love, we simultaneously hate, idolize, and exploit the bodies of others.

[154] Cited in S. L. Jones and M. A Yarhouse, *Homosexuality: The Use of Scientific Research in the Church's Moral Debate* (Downers Grove, IL: InterVarsity Press, 2000), 153.

[155] The same ambiguity of language is true with regard to "natural." All sin is "natural" and "unnatural" depending on whether you are talking about fallen or unfallen nature. Another important distinction is that between "natural" meaning "that which accords with the *telos* or true purpose of a given creature," and "natural" meaning "a state of affairs which exists." The first of these is assumed in this chapter (sin is unnatural in so far as it represents a rejection of God's purposes for humankind). The second is the root of the "naturalistic," or "is-ought," fallacy.

[156] The relevance of this passage is pointed out by Bledsoe in his lectures, "Envy, Scapegoating and Neurosis."

[157] The next two paragraphs are almost entirely dependent upon Bledsoe's comments in "Envy, Scapegoating and Neurosis." He explores these themes at much greater length and with illustrations and confirmation from classical literature and from Scripture.

[158] It is not surprising that one of the most convincing Christ-figures in modern literature, Carlo in Louis de Berniere's fiercely anti-Christian *Captain Corelli's Mandolin*, is a homosexual. Examples could be multiplied.

[159] The relationship between persecution, victimhood, and masochism is complex, but the idea that the self-hating sinner will begin punishing himself if others do not punish him makes theological – and therefore psychological – sense.

[160] Bledsoe, "Envy, Scapegoating and Neurosis."

[161] Hilary of Poitiers, *De Trinitate*, 3.21.

[162] Jenson, *Systematic Theology*, 2:146.

[163] Pannenberg, "Revelation and Homosexual Experience," 37.

[164] Hays, *Moral Vision*, 389.

[165] All cited by R. J. Neuhaus in "In the Case of John Boswell," *First Things* 41 (March 1994), 56–59. Also at: http://www.first-things.com/ftissues/ft9403/public.html.

[166] Jenson, *Systematic Theology*, 2:147.

[167] Satinover, *Homosexuality*, 47.

[168] *Moral Evasion* (London: Centre for Policy Studies, 1998). Selbourne's thesis is that relativists have given up responding to assertions of common moral rules with arguments and have instead devised a number of evasions, which are used to undermine the possibility of argument itself. His booklet lists eleven of these: "there is nothing you can do about it, or not much"; "it has never been any different"; "there is no quick fix" for a given ethical dilemma; "this is the price of a free society"; "you must move with the tide"; "there is no use turning the clock back"; the problem is "much more complex than you think"; "it's beyond the reach of the law"; "you are focussing on the wrong issue"; "people in glass houses shouldn't . . ."; "who are you to talk?"

and the basic evasion that, since "everyone does it," how can you object?

[169] Muller's comments on the work of Judith Butler and Michel Foucault highlight the not unrelated alliance between gay activism, feminist lesbianism, and postmodern pluralism: "For Foucault there is no such thing as legitimate authority, there is only 'power,' and the most insidious form of power is self-discipline, which comes from having internalized standards of normalcy from social institutions" ("Coming Out Ahead").

[170] J. Nicolosi, "The Gay Deception," in *Homosexuality*, ed. Wolfe, 98–105 (p. 102).

[171] J. O'Connor and J. Seymour, *Introducing NLP* (London: HarperCollins, 1993), 78–80.

[172] Hays, *Moral Vision*, 379.

[173] For E. Moberley, see "Homosexuality and the Truth," *First Things* 71 (March 1997): 30–33. For Fitzgibbons and Nicolosi see Wolfe, ed., *Homosexuality*.

[174] Greenberg, *Construction of Homosexuality*, 489. Ironically, in the light of the efforts of so much gay activism to identify a person with his sexual orientation, Foucault, an existentialist in this, rejects the view that homosexuality is "constituted . . . less by a type of sexual relations than by a certain quality of sexual sensibility" (*History of Sexuality*, 43).

[175] Cited by Nicolosi, "The Gay Deception," 101. See also R. J. Rushdoony, *Institutes of Biblical Law*, I (Phillipsburg, PA: Presbyterian and Reformed, 1973), 419–27. Muller summarizes Judith Butler on this point: "The 'foundational categories of identity' that make heterosexual behavior and desire appear natural and inevitable are to be unmasked as 'performances', which are a product of culture rather than of nature" ("Coming Out Ahead").

[176] Cited by Satinover, *Homosexuality*, 199. See also O'Donovan in *Theology and Sexuality*, ed. Rogers, 380–81.

[177] In Wolfe, ed., *Homosexuality*, 102.

[178] Hays, *Moral Vision*, 391.

179 Hays, *Moral Vision*, 390.

180 Jones and Yarhouse, *Homosexuality*, 181.

181 C. Van Til, *The Defense of the Faith*, rev. ed. (Philadelphia: Presbyterian and Reformed, 1963) and *A Christian Theory of Knowledge* (Nutley, NJ: Presbyterian and Reformed, 1969); J. Frame, *Cornelius Van Til: An Analysis of His Thought* (Phillipsburg, PA: Presbyterian and Reformed, 1995); R. J. Rushdoony, *By What Standard? An Analysis of the Philosophy of Cornelius Van Til* (Philadelphia: Presbyterian and Reformed, 1965).

182 In this sense there is a circularity in comments upon the "essence" of sin. J. B. De Young, for example, writes on consecutive pages that "Pride is the essence of all sin" and "The essence of the error of homosexuality is pride" (*Homosexuality: Contemporary Claims Examined in Light of the Bible and Other Ancient Literature and Law* [Grand Rapids, MI: Kregel Publications, 2000], 15–16).

183 This understanding, therefore, recognizes that "essentialism" and "constructionism" are not so mutually exclusive as is sometimes thought.

184 S. Joel Garver, of LaSalle University, in private correspondence.

185 J. Satinover, "The Biology of Homosexuality: Science or Politics?" in *Homosexuality*, ed. Wolfe, 13. See also, illustratively, O'Donovan's discussion of "the homosexual phenomenon" and the way that he chooses to differentiate "gay" and "homosexual," in "Homosexuality in the Church: Can There Be a Fruitful Theological Debate?" in *Theology and Sexuality*, ed. Rogers, 373–86 (pp. 377–78).

186 For example, Gagnon summarizes David Greenberg's categorization: transgenerational; transgenderal; class-structured; and egalitarian, in *The Bible and Homosexual Practice*, 414.

187 Robert Jenson makes an interesting attempt at answering this in *Systematic Theology*, 2:88–89, although it is an answer which incorporates his conclusions regarding the Christian stance towards homoerotic acts. See also Michel Foucault, *History of Sexuality*.

188 Andrew McComiskey, cited in Satinover, *Homosexuality*, 202.

189 Quoted in P. Jewett, *Who We Are: Our Dignity as Human: A Neo-evangelical Theology* (Grand Rapids, MI: Eerdmans, 1996), 299–300.

190 Jenson, *Systematic Theology*, 2:138, 141, 145, 148.

191 Peter Saunders, *Homosexuality*, in CMF Files 20(May 2003): 1. http://www.cmf.org.uk/cmffiles/pdffiles/homosex.pdf.

192 McCarthy, "The Relationship of Bodies," 212.

193 Hays, *Moral Vision*, 388. Gagnon significantly qualifies this understanding, however, in *The Bible and Homosexual Practice*, 347–60, 380–95.

194 *History of Sexuality*, 43. David Greenberg's *The Construction of Homosexuality* is a standard reference on these matters.

195 Gagnon gets close to this, moving from the Bible's "relative disinterest" to speaking of behaviors as being "what matters" (pp. 37–38; see also 380–91). Note also the title of his book, *The Bible and Homosexual Practice*. Robert Jenson claims that "the question of whether there are 'orientations' and of how they occur if there are such is an empirical question, from the solution of which nothing whatever follows ethically or theologically" (*Systematic Theology*, 2:141, note 36).

196 Satinover, "Biology," 12.

197 Hays, *Moral Vision*, 390. See also Paul Jewett's remark: "Even if it were demonstrated beyond any possible doubt that homosexuality is determined either entirely biologically or by some combination of biological and social factors outside an individual's control, that does not, ipso facto, remove it from the realm of moral judgment" (*Who We Are*, 349).

198 "The Homosexual Movement: A Response." As it stands, this statement requires qualification. Inclination to sin is not sinful in the sense of being a sinful *act*, but as a manifestation of a corrupt nature it is evil. Canon XI of the *Formula Consensus Helvetica (1675)* states that "man, because of sin, is by nature, and hence from his birth, before committing any actual sin, exposed to God's wrath and curse; first, on account of the

transgression and disobedience which he committed in the loins of Adam; and, secondly, on account of the consequent hereditary corruption implanted to his very conception, whereby his whole nature is depraved and spiritually dead; so that original sin may rightly be regarded as twofold, imputed sin and inherent hereditary sin." The full text can be found in M. I. Klauber, "The Helvetic Formula Consensus (1675): An Introduction and Translation," *Trinity Journal* (1990): 103–23. I am immensely grateful to my colleague Dr. Garry J. Williams, both for bringing this to my attention and also for insight relating to a number of points in this and subsequent paragraphs.

[199] A. Whyte, *Samuel Rutherford and Some of His Correspondents* (Edinburgh: Oliphant Anderson & Ferrier, 1894), 56. The "dangerous doxologies" are, of course, Augustine's "*beata culpa*" (blessed fault), and Gregory's "*felix culpa*" (happy fault). George Fox declared, "My sins have in a manner done me more good than my graces" and James Fraser noted, "I find advantage of my sins."

[200] Oliver O'Donovan explores rather different ideas of homosexual "vocation" in "Homosexuality in the Church." In this discussion he allows for the possibility of homosexual sexual activity for reasons of "pastoral expediency" (p. 383). He also suggests that understanding homosexual relationships within an "affective friendship model" rather than a "marriage model" might lead to homosexual sexual activity in such relationships being judged "indulgently" (p. 384).

[201] A. Bonar, ed., *Letters of Samuel Rutherford* (Edinburgh: Banner of Truth Trust, 1984), letter CLVII.

[202] One example, from Richard Baxter's *A Christian Directory*, in *The Practical Works of Richard Baxter* (Morgan, PA: Soli Deo Gloria, 2000) is given as the appendix to this chapter and repays a close reading.

[203] The questions which this raises about why Adam sinned, in what ways Christ's temptations were the "same" as ours (Heb. 2) and in what ways different, and the liability to punishment of

those who do not have "opportunity" for their fallen nature to come to fruition, such as infants dying in infancy, cannot be explored here.

[204] Jones and Yarhouse, *Homosexuality*, 179.

[205] Jones and Yarhouse, *Homosexuality*, 181.

[206] Deut. 32:35. Let readers of Jonathan Edwards understand.

[207] R. B. Martin, *Gerard Manley Hopkins: A Very Private Life* (London: Flamingo, 1992).

[208] This passage is from Baxter's *A Christian Directory*, I. II. vii, vol. 1, 222–23.

[209] There is a network of similar organizations affiliated with Exodus International in Europe, North America, Latin America, and the South Pacific.

[210] An earlier version of this article appeared in B. Edwards, ed., *Homosexuality: The Straight Agenda* (Epsom: DayOne, 1998), 53–74. It is reprinted in this revised form with the permission of the original publisher.

[211] J. Bancroft, "Homosexual Orientation: The Search for a Biological Basis," *British Journal of Psychiatry* 164 (1994): 437–40 (p. 439).

[212] A. Kinsey, et al., *Sexual Behavior in the Human Male* (Philadelphia: W. B. Saunders, 1948).

[213] C. Socarides and B. Kauffman, "Reparative Therapy (letter)," *American Journal of Psychiatry* 151 (1994): 157–59.

[214] Bancroft, "Homosexual Orientation," 439.

[215] U. Schuklenk and M. Ristow, "The Ethics of Research into the Cause(s) of Homosexuality," *Journal of Homosexuality* 31, no. 3 (1996): 5–30.

[216] W. Byne and E. Stein, "Ethical Implications of Scientific Research on the Causes of Sexual Orientation," *Health Care Analysis 5*, no. 2 (1997): 136–48.

[217] R. Green, "The Immutability of (Homo)sexual Orientation: Behavioral Science Implications of a Constitutional (Legal) Analysis," *Journal of Psychiatry and Law* (winter 1988): 537–75.

[218] M. Bailey and R. Pillard, in *Opinions and Editorials, New York Times* (Dec. 17, 1991): 19.

[219] A. Bell, et al., *Sexual Preference: Its Development in Men and Women* (Bloomington, IN: Indiana University Press, 1981), 219.

[220] F. Muscarella, "The Evolution of Homoerotic Behavior in Humans," *Journal of Homosexuality* 40, no. 1 (2000): 51–77. This article supposedly explains why homosexuals have an adaptive advantage.

[221] D. Altman, *The Homosexualisation of America* (Boston: Beacon Press, 1982); M. Kirk and H. Madsen, *After the Ball* (New York: Doubleday, 1989).

[222] T. Landess, "Gay Rights in America: The Ultimate PR Campaign," *Rutherford Journal* 3, no. 7 (1994): 3–11.

[223] Kinsey, et al., *Sexual Behavior*.

[224] A. Johnson, et el., *Sexual Attitudes and Lifestyle* (Oxford: Blackwell Scientific, 1994), cited by A. Tonks, "British Sex Survey Shows Popularity of Monogamy," *British Medical Journal* 308 (1994): 209.

[225] A. M. Johnson, et al., "Sexual Behavior in Britain: Partnerships, Practices, and HIV Risk Behaviors," *The Lancet* 358 (2001): 1835–42.

[226] D. Hamer, et al., "A Linkage Between DNA Markers on the X Chromosome and Male Sexual Orientation," *Science* 261 (1993): 321–27.

[227] M. Baron, "Genetic Linkage and Male Homosexual Orientation," *British Medical Journal* 307 (1993): 337–38.

[228] J. Bailey and R. Pillard, "A Genetic Study of Male Sexual Orientation," *Archives of General Psychiatry* 48 (1991): 1089–96.

[229] R. Pillard and M. Bailey, "A Biologic Perspective of Heterosexual, Bisexual and Homosexual Behavior," *Psychiatric Clinics of North America* 18, no. 1 (1995): 71–84.

[230] P. Van Wyk and C. Geist, "Psychosocial Development of Heterosexual, Bisexual and Homosexual Behavior," *Archives of Sexual Behaviour* 13 (1984): 505–44.

[231] H. Meyer-Bahlburg, "Psychoendocrine Research on Sexual Orientation: Current Status and Future Options," *Progress in Brain Research* 61 (1984): 375–98.

[232] R. Goy and B. McEwen, *Sexual Differentiation of the Brain* (Cambridge, MA: MIT Press, 1980).

[233] H. Meyer-Bahlburg, "Sex Hormones and Male Homosexuality in Comparative Perspective," *Archives of Sexual Behaviour* 6 (1977): 297–325.

[234] H. Meyer-Bahlburg, "Sex Hormones and Female Sexuality: A Critical Examination," *Archives of Sexual Behaviour* 8 (1979): 101–19; W. Byne and B. Parsons, "Human Sexual Orientation: The Biologic Theories Reappraised," *Archives of General Psychiatry* 50 (1993): 228–39. See also Pillard and Bailey, "A Biologic Perspective."

[235] Cf. Byne and Parsons, "Human Sexual Orientation."

[236] J. Money, et al., "Adult Heterosexual Status and Fetal Hormonal Masculinisation," *Psychoneuroendocrinology* 9 (1984): 405–14.

[237] D. Swaab and E. Fliers, "A Sexually Dimorphic Nucleus in the Human Brain," *Science* 228 (1985): 1112–14.

[238] D. Swaab and M. Hoffman, "Sexual Differentiation of the Human Hypothalamus: Ontogeny of the Sexually Dimorphic Nucleus of the Preoptic Area," *Developmental Brain Research* 44 (1988): 314–18.

[239] S. LeVay, "A Difference in Hypothalamic Structure Between Heterosexual and Homosexual Men," *Science* 253 (1991): 1034–37. LeVay measured postmortem tissue from three subject groups: women, men who were presumed to be heterosexual, and homosexual men.

[240] Cf. Byne and Parsons, "Human Sexual Orientation."

[241] W. Byne, et al., "The Interstitial Nuclei of the Human Anterior Hypothalamus: An Investigation of Sexual Variation in Volume and Cell Size, Number and Density," *Brain Research* 856, nos. 1–2 (2000): 254–58.

[242] L. Allen and R. Gorski, "Sexual Orientation and the Size of the Anterior Commissure in the Human Brain," *Proceedings of the National Academy of Sciences*, USA 891 (1992): 7199–7202.

243 M. S. Lasco, et al., "A Lack of Dimorphism of Sex or Sexual Orientation in the Human Anterior Commissure," *Brain Research* 936 (2002): 95–98.

244 Cf. Byne and Parsons, "Human Sexual Orientation," 235.

245 F. Kallman, "Comparative Twin Study of the Genetic Aspects of Homósexuality," *Journal of Nervous and Mental Disease* 115 (1952): 288–98.

246 J. Bailey and R. Pillard, "A Genetic Study of Male Sexual Orientation," *Archives of General Psychiatry* 48 (1991): 1089–96.

247 J. Bailey, et al., "Heritable Factors Influence Sexual Orientation in Women," *Archives of General Psychiatry* 50 (1993): 217–23.

248 E. Eckert, et al., "Homosexuality in Monozygotic Twins Reared Apart," *British Journal of Psychiatry* 148 (1986): 421–25.

249 T. McGuire, "Is Homosexuality Genetic? A Critical Review and Some Suggestions," *Journal of Homosexuality* 28, nos.1–2 (1995): 115–45.

250 Cf. Hamer, et al., "A Linkage."

251 Cf. Baron, "Genetic Linkage and Male Homosexual Orientation."

252 M. King, "Sexual Orientation and the X," *Nature* 364 (1993): 228–29.

253 McGuire, "Is Homosexuality Genetic?"

254 G. Rice, et al., "Male Homosexuality: Absence of Linkage to Microsatellite Markers at Xq28," *Science* 284 (1999): 665–67.

255 L. Thompson, "Search for a Gay Gene," *Time* (12 June 1995): 52–53.

256 W. Masters and V. Johnson, *Homosexuality in Perspective* (Boston: Little, Brown & Co., 1979).

257 R. L. Spitzer, "Can Some Gay Men and Lesbians Change Their Sexual Orientation? 200 Participants Reporting a Change from Homosexual to Heterosexual Orientation," *Archives of Sexual Behavior* 32, no. 5 (2003): 403–17; discussion 419–72.

258 Cf. McGuire, "Is Homosexuality Genetic?"

[259] K. S. Kendler, et al., "Sexual Orientation in a U.S. National Sample of Twin and Nontwin Sibling Pairs," *American Journal of Psychiatry* 157 (2000): 1843–46.

[260] C. Cloninger, "A Systematic Method for Clinical Description and Classification of Personality Variants," *Archives of General Psychiatry* 44 (1987): 573–88.

[261] Cf. Bancroft, "Homosexual Orientation," 439.

[262] Bell, et al., *Sexual Preference*, 41–62; 117–34.

[263] E. Moberley, "Homosexuality: Structure and Evaluation," *Theology* 83 (1980): 177–84.

[264] www.truefreedomtrust.co.uk.

[265] M. Hallett, "Homosexuality," *Nucleus* (Jan. 1994): 14–19.

[266] S. Lawton, "Key Issues in Counselling Lesbians: Counselling those Struggling with Homosexuality and Lesbianism – A Christian Approach," Signposts to Wholeness Conference, True freedom Trust, 1994.

[267] M. Saghir and E. Robins, *Male and Female Homosexuality: A Comprehensive Investigation* (Baltimore, MD: Williams Wilkins, 1973).

[268] Cloninger, "A Systematic Method."

[269] R. Friedman, *Male Homosexuality: A Contemporary Psychoanalytical Perspective* (New Haven, CT: Yale University Press, 1988), 33–48.

[270] T. Schmidt, *Straight and Narrow? Compassion and Clarity in the Homosexuality Debate* (Leicester: IVP, 1995), 215.

[271] Bancroft, "Homosexual Orientation," 439.

[272] Adapted from Schmidt, *Straight and Narrow?*, 51.

[273] S. Jones and M. Yarhouse, "What Causes Homosexuality?," in *Homosexuality: The Use of Scientific Research in the Church's Moral Debate*, 47–91; Schmidt, "The Great Nature-Nurture Debate," in *Straight and Narrow?*, 131–59; P. Saunders, CMF Files 20, *Homosexuality*.

[274] P. Saunders and R. Pickering, "Homosexuality: The Causes," *Nucleus* (Oct. 1997): 19–28; P. Saunders, "Just Genetics?" in *Homosexuality*, ed. Edwards, 53–74.